The American West: A Very Short Introduction

VERY SHORT INTRODUCTIONS are for anyone wanting a stimulating and accessible way into a new subject. They are written by experts and have been translated into more than 40 different languages.

The series began in 1995 and now covers a wide variety of topics in every discipline. The VSI library now contains more than 400 volumes—a Very Short Introduction to everything from Indian philosophy to psychology and American History—and continues to grow in every subject area.

Very Short Introductions available now:

For more information visit our web site

www.oup.com/vsi/

Stephen Aron

THE AMERICAN WEST

A Very Short Introduction

OXFORD
UNIVERSITY PRESS

OXFORD
UNIVERSITY PRESS

Oxford University Press is a department of the
University of Oxford. It furthers the University's objective
of excellence in research, scholarship, and education
by publishing worldwide.

Oxford   New York

Auckland   Cape Town   Dar es Salaam   Hong Kong   Karachi
Kuala Lumpur   Madrid   Melbourne   Mexico City   Nairobi
New Delhi   Shanghai   Taipei   Toronto

With offices in

Argentina   Austria   Brazil   Chile   Czech Republic   France   Greece
Guatemala   Hungary   Italy   Japan   Poland   Portugal   Singapore
South Korea   Switzerland   Thailand   Turkey   Ukraine   Vietnam

Oxford is a registered trade mark of Oxford University Press
in the UK and certain other countries.

Published in the United States of America by
Oxford University Press
198 Madison Avenue, New York, NY 10016

Library of Congress Cataloging-in-Publication Data
has been applied for

ISBN 978-0-19-985893-4

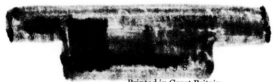

Printed in Great Britain
by Ashford Colour Press Ltd., Gosport, Hants.
on acid-free paper

*For my teachers: Robert Gross, Charles Sellers,
John Murrin, and John Gray*

Contents

List of illustrations

Acknowledgments

This is a "Very Short Introduction," but it has benefited from a long list of listeners and readers. In the first category are thousands of undergraduates and dozens of graduate students who were captivated or perhaps just captives as I worked out ideas and themes in this book over the twenty plus years that I have been teaching the history of the American West at Princeton University and UCLA. My thanks to them, to my colleagues at UCLA and the Autry National Center, and especially to David Myers, the current chair of the history department at UCLA. I am also very grateful to the many readers who tackled earlier versions of the manuscript and offered immensely valuable comments and corrections: Adam Arenson, Marilyn Aron, Paul Aron, Eric Avila, Katherine Benton-Cohen, John Bowes, Meredith Mason Brown, Carolyn Brucken, Lawrence Culver, Matthew Dennis, William Deverell, John Mack Faragher, Amy Green, Erik Greenberg, John Gray, Andrew Graybill, David Igler, Kelly Lytle-Hernandez, Benjamin Madley, Joshua Paddison, David Paddy, Erika Perez, Malcolm Rohrbough, Arthur Rolston, Virginia Scharff, Rachel St. John, Brenda Stevenson, Allison Varzally, and Karen Wilson. Thanks as well to Marva Felchlin for helping me find the images and to Nancy Toff, Rebecca Hecht, and Martha Ramsey for their keen editorial judgments.

The book is dedicated to four extraordinary mentors, none of whom is a historian of the American West, but what they taught me about history shapes this book.

Introduction:
American Wests

"This is the West, sir. When the legend becomes fact, print the legend." So the journalist, Maxwell Scott, tells the senator, Ransom Stoddard, at the end of *The Man Who Shot Liberty Valance*, a 1962 Western directed by John Ford. It has become one of the most quoted movie lines, and its message resonates through the pages of this book. As Jimmy Stewart's Stoddard learned, the confusion of legend and fact, of myth and history, makes it hard to disentangle the stories we have told about the development of the American West from our understanding of what really happened. This book explains how the gap between projections and reality has shaped the development of the West and confounded our interpretations of its history. Owing to the ubiquity of popular representations (and misrepresentations) in movies, television series, novels, songs, and paintings, many readers come to this volume with firm yet false ideas about the West and its past. These perceptions make for a history that is too short, too small, too simple, and too singular.

To correct for the truncated vision of Westerns, this history of the American West stretches the chronology, enlarges the geography, complicates the casting, and pluralizes the subject. Where Westerns typically take place over the course of a few decades after the Civil War, this book opens up a much longer history. It begins hundreds of years before the West was American; it does not halt, as so many Westerns have, with the supposed "closing of the frontier" at the end of the nineteenth century but continues through the twentieth century and into the twenty-first. In addition, unlike Westerns, in which certain landscapes have been favored settings, this survey takes a more expansive view. The West as we know it today (more or less the western half of the United States) is not the West as earlier generations mapped it. Not that long ago, from the point of view of Europeans, all of North America was the West. Still longer ago, for most of the people who lived there it was not a West at all. How portions of North America became Wests, how parts of these became American, and how American Wests ultimately became the American West are central questions in this book.

Answers, though, are not so straightforward. The maps that earlier generations used (some essentially still in use today), first to divvy up North America and later to mark the Wests of the United States, were cartographic fantasies, presuming to erect walls in places where there were no true foundations yet—or at best very shaky ones. These competing colonial projections failed to respect the claims of Indian peoples or to reflect the intricacies of interpersonal, intercultural, and international relations on the ground. Even after various Wests were incorporated into the United States, the national orientation of these territories remained contested, subject to challenges from rival claimants. Indeed, in recent times as in the deeper past, efforts to occupy and pursuits of opportunity have brought diverse peoples to and through multiple Wests. Across the centuries, the movements of peoples and the minglings of cultures have shaped the history of sharp confrontations and murky convergences that unfolds in the pages that follow.

Chapter 1
The view from Cahokia

The Gateway Arch in St. Louis is an appropriate perch from which to begin a contemplation of the history of American Wests. The monument was designed to celebrate the westward expansion of the United States and to place St. Louis at its opening. On a clear day, from the top of this edifice more than six hundred feet up, the view to the west dazzles.

Yet the history of Wests requires viewers to take in the entire panorama. While facing east, they might consider the American West that once stretched that way from the Mississippi River. Gazing east, they might also imagine how the landscape looked long before there was a United States or even a St. Louis. With that deeper historical view, the great earthen mounds of Cahokia would dominate the immediate horizon.

Nine hundred years ago, those mounds stood at the center of the largest metropolis in what is now the United States. Cahokia's influence reached across a vast hinterland. Products flowed to it from all directions. People came to it from afar. And then, for reasons we do not completely understand, Cahokia was abandoned. Its mounds were eroding by the time Europeans arrived in the area.

Much remains a mystery about Cahokia (including what its inhabitants called it) and about Indian words and worlds in the centuries before Europeans envisioned the Americas as their West. From the vantage point of Cahokia unfolds not a static and generic "prehistory" but a dynamic and diverse past defined by peoples in motion, societies in flux, cultures entangling, powers competing, and realms shifting—all with important implications for the colonial trajectories that followed.

The local view

Mounds made of packed earth first appeared in and around the confluence of the Mississippi and Missouri Rivers around one thousand years ago. Thousands more elevations, mostly in the form of cones and pyramids, but also in a variety of animal shapes, could be found from the Great Plains to the Atlantic Ocean and from the Great Lakes to the Gulf of Mexico. Mounds were particularly abundant in the Mississippi and Ohio valleys, where the construction of some dated back thousands of years, and where what historians call "Mississippian culture" flourished between AD 900 and 1300.

Cahokia boasted the most impressive constellation of mounds. There some 120 mounds, spread across five square miles, had been built by AD 1100. The largest of these pyramids, which we know as Monk's Mound, covered fifteen acres, contained twenty-two million cubic feet of dirt, and ascended in three terraces to a platform one hundred feet above the base. A fifty-acre rectangular plaza stretched in front of it. On top of Monk's and other mounds were staged a variety of rituals and ceremonies witnessed by multitudes on the plazas below. Between the mounds, plazas and residential quarters housed between ten and twenty thousand people at their peak in the twelfth century. Beyond were immense fields that provided the basic subsistence of the largest congregation of inhabitants north of Mexico.

Feeding so many mouths and building so many mounds were enormous and elaborate undertakings. In normal times, Cahokians, like residents of other Mississippian settlements, drew their subsistence from a combination of hunting, fishing, gathering, and, above all, farming. The latter, which mixed together the cultivation of maize, beans, and squash, was principally the responsibility of women, and it was the most important contributor to Mississippian diets. While the basic technology for cultivating these crops remained simple—sticks to make holes to plant seeds and stone hoes to build up hills around plants—the development of new strains of corn, better suited to colder climates and shorter growing seasons, was essential to the success of farmers at Cahokia and across the woodlands of North America. Absent from diets here and throughout precolonial Indian America were meat and milk from livestock, for the Americas never had or had long lost larger animals suitable for domestication. The lack of sizeable beasts of burden also meant that all of the dirt for all of the mounds had to be carried by humans alone. One basket at a time, it took more than three million hours of human labor to construct Monk's Mound.

These mounds required that builders be at least partially freed from the demands of food production. Fortunately, during the several hundred years that coincided with Cahokia's heyday, food was produced easily enough and in sufficient quantities. In these centuries, Cahokians, other Mississippians, and indeed Indians across a good part of North America profited from favorable climate change. Beginning around AD 800 and continuing for around four hundred years, the climate across much of the Northern Hemisphere became wetter and warmer. Longer growing seasons and more predictable rainfall improved yields and permitted agriculture to spread into new regions.

Cahokians benefited as well from far-reaching exchange networks. Drawing resources from distant places was no recent development. Excavations of much older sites in mid-America have uncovered shells from the Gulf of Mexico, copper from the Great Lakes, and obsidian from the Rockies. But no other Mississippian site has revealed a network as vast or extensive as at Cahokia.

Why these items came in such quantities to Cahokia is a subject of debate. Archaeologists generally believe that much of the flow owed to Cahokia's place as a religious and imperial center and was tribute from subordinated peoples. Deer remains found at Cahokia, which include few lower limb, skull, or neck bones, have led archaeologists to the conclusion that the animals were likely killed elsewhere than Cahokia and only prime cuts were transported there. Burial practices provide additional confirmation of social hierarchies in Cahokia and between it and its hinterlands. How else to explain the presence of vast quantities of exotic goods, often carefully laid out in the form of an animal, in the graves of a favored few? Not just goods, but also other people were interred alongside these presumably high-status individuals. Many of these skeletons, sometimes numbering in the dozens and typically young women, displayed signs of malnourishment and ritual mutilation, which suggests that they were enslaved captives who were sacrificed during funeral ceremonies.

If some people in Cahokia's expansive orbit acceded to the supremacy of the center, others resisted its domination. In the former category were those villages (generally in the vicinity of Cahokia but some at a greater distance) where Cahokian ways, rites, and symbols blended with or replaced indigenous cultural elements. Yet even in these places, demands from Cahokia's imperial-religious masters seem to have generated resentments. Whether such anger turned into armed clashes is not clear, though in the third quarter of the twelfth century, Cahokians built a two-mile palisade around the central city to protect against attackers. In these same years and in ensuing decades, warfare appears to have become more frequent.

Mounting defense costs contributed to Cahokia's decline in the thirteenth century, but environmental changes proved more devastating. To be sure, a connection existed between the two. The palisades, for example, required thousands of logs to construct, and cutting so many trees exacerbated shortages of wood. Deforestation, in turn, left fields more vulnerable to flooding and soil erosion, which reduced harvests and brought food scarcity where there had been surplus. An even greater challenge to the well-being of Cahokians came from climate changes that affected peoples across much of the globe. After several hundred years of generally wetter and warmer times, coinciding with Cahokia's rise, in the thirteenth century came a prolonged period in which the climate grew colder and rainfall less consistent. The "Little Ice Age" shortened growing seasons on both sides of the north Atlantic, disrupting long-standing agricultural practices and forcing farmers to change their ways. Some of Cahokia's neighbors adapted more readily by planting new varieties of corn. By contrast, Cahokia's growers kept closer to custom and experienced diminishing harvests.

As food supplies decreased and other necessities, such as game and timber, became harder to find, the glory days of Cahokia faded. By 1200, its population was probably half of what it had once been. Fifty years later only around two thousand people were there. Through the remainder of the thirteenth century, the population continued to fall. No single catastrophe seems to have occurred to cause this decline. Emigration—not starvation— appears to have reduced Cahokia's population. By around 1400, Cahokia had been entirely depopulated, its magnificent mounds abandoned.

The continental view

Exceptional as the rise and fall of Cahokia was, it exemplifies more general rules about the history of precolonial North America (which for the purposes of this book refers only to that portion of

North America that is north of present-day Mexico). True, Cahokia's mounds were taller and more numerous, its population many times larger, its radius much wider than any other Mississippian site, or any metropolis north of Mexico. To survey precolonial American history exclusively from Cahokia would be akin to treating a study of Paris or London in the Middle Ages as a stand-in for all of medieval Europe. Still, in the case of Cahokia, the differences between it and its hinterlands were more a matter of degree than of kind.

Unlike the European cities to which its population compared, Cahokia lacked the administrative apparatus and occupational distinctions of those capitals. It developed no imperial bureaucracy or standing army. Nor, despite Cahokia's extensive exchange relations, did its population include a distinct set of merchants. In contrast with European towns, Cahokia also had no specialized artisans. Instead, people farmed. More specifically, women cultivated, with assistance from men. Cahokia's men, like Indian men across much of North America, supplemented the foods produced and prepared primarily by women by hunting and fishing. In between these activities, they engaged in the raids that brought captives to Cahokia and demonstrated their worthiness as warriors.

Such patterns of life and labor came to characterize Indian societies across those portions of North America where maize-growing took hold. The correspondences were most obvious in other Mississippian towns, which established their own chiefdoms with expansive trading and raiding networks, featured similarly built-to-awe mounds, and venerated corn for its life-giving qualities. Like Cahokia, the inhabitants of these sites suffered as well when climate change cut harvests and intensified competition for vital resources. In the face of prolonged difficult times, they, too, likely doubted the spiritual powers on which the authority of rulers rested. Under environmental and human pressure, some chiefdoms collapsed completely during the thirteenth and fourteenth centuries; other Mississippian towns hung on, albeit in much reduced states.

In the metropolis of Cahokia and in small Mississippian villages, daily existence and rituals were quite similar because of the common denominator of corn. Although it had taken thousands of years for the cultivation of maize to spread from its Mesoamerican points of origin into North America, its realm expanded far more quickly during the favorable climatic period that coincided with Cahokia's rise. Crossing longitudinal lines much more readily than it had during its long northward march from Mexico, maize had come by AD 1000 or 1100 to supply the foundations of subsistence for most peoples across the eastern woodlands (at least south of the Great Lakes). Its cultivators also pushed westward from the Mississippi River onto the eastern plains. When corn gained primacy, it not only fed people but also suffused the stories they told about their origins, inspired the ceremonies they performed to keep their worlds in order, and reshaped the roles and powers of men and women.

In addition, as at Cahokia, when corn-growing became more difficult, the problem created social instability in societies and promoted more violence between them. One response, of which the archaeological record provides abundant evidence, was to abandon fields (and villages) in no longer productive areas and seek opportunities elsewhere. Another was to fight over suddenly more scarce resources. That seems to explain an attack in the early fourteenth century on a community along the Missouri River in present-day South Dakota. The victims, who numbered nearly five hundred men, women, and children, were already malnourished when their enemies, possibly in the same condition, burned their fortified settlement and mutilated its inhabitants.

The closest parallel to Cahokia's rise and fall was in Chaco Canyon in northwestern New Mexico. Around the same time that Cahokia and other Mississippian sites were taking off, the people of Chaco (whose name for themselves we also do not know, but whose enemies referred to them as the Anasazi) were expanding their settlements. By the end of the eleventh century, a dozen towns and scores of smaller hamlets dotted the canyon floor and the surrounding area (now the Four Corners region where New Mexico, Arizona, Utah, and Colorado converge), which was home to several thousand people. Most impressive was what is now known as Pueblo Bonita. There the edifices that inspired awe were not earthen mounds but multistory buildings, which, like Cahokia's pyramids, required the marshaling of an immense labor force. Approximately one million dressed stones were used in the buildings at Pueblo Bonita, along with two hundred thousand logs, most of them transported more than forty miles into the canyon. As at Cahokia, none of this would have been possible without a large workforce and an ample food supply. These existed, because the people of Chaco Canyon had learned to grow corn. Indeed, Chaco was closer to Mexico, and corn had come earlier there than to Cahokia. But in the more arid environment of Chaco, its successful cultivation necessitated the construction of an elaborate complex of dams, ditches, canals, and reservoirs to keep fields sufficiently watered. In addition to the waterworks, the people of Chaco also built hundreds of miles of roads to connect their towns and to foster the movement of goods and people in and out of the canyon.

This system functioned well for several hundred years—until fifty years of drought struck, beginning around 1130. Prayers for rain went unanswered, and storehouses of corn were depleted. Population declined, and some communities were abandoned. During the thirteenth and fourteenth centuries, the drier climate and the downward trends continued. Competition once again bred increased warfare and decreased quality of life. As had happened at Cahokia, the descendants of those who had built Pueblo Bonita and other sites in Chaco Canyon and its vicinity ultimately gave up and moved on.

Where did they go? The most common supposition is to the Rio Grande Valley, where they became the progenitors of the Pueblo peoples. A few centuries later, the region the Anasazi (or Ancestral Pueblo peoples) had left was resettled by migrants who had journeyed into the Four Corners region from previous homes a thousand or so miles to the north and west. These newcomers split into the Navajos and the Apaches, extending their domains around the Pueblo towns and territories. A new world developed in the aftermath of Chaco Canyon's demise, one whose trajectory would be profoundly altered when newer comers arrived from the south at the end of the seventeenth century.

The comparative view

Moving around was a time-tested survival strategy for Indians across North America. Even relatively settled farming peoples undertook seasonal migrations in search of wild game to supplement their agricultural production. When resources were exhausted, more permanent relocations, as at Cahokia and Chaco Canyon, occurred. For nonfarming peoples, whose territory still encompassed the majority of North America, itinerancy was essential. While favorable climate shifts permitted the expansion of corn's realm, the crop still required a 120-day growing season, which excluded most of Canada. It also needed approximately twenty inches of rain spread across the year—or, barring that, a major manipulation of water supplies as at Chaco Canyon. Most of the western half of North America lacked that amount of rain, and very few of the societies that developed were inclined or organized to carry out significant irrigation projects. The more mobile societies that inhabited the west and the far north of North America relied exclusively on hunting, fishing, and gathering. These modes of subsistence and the mobility they required add to the remarkable diversity of Indian America and further differentiated societies on the western side of the north Atlantic from those on its eastern flank.

During the colonial era, Europeans conceived a ladder of cultural development that assigned the top rung to those with dense sedentary populations and expansive trade networks. Europeans also deemed agriculture an essential mark of improvement. At the bottom of this hierarchy were hunter-gatherers. Through this lens, which has continued to influence evaluations of human progress, Cahokia and Pueblo Bonita earn pride of place among Indian societies of precolonial North America. By contrast, more nomadic hunting bands get designated primitive and static.

In fact, these Indians, like those at Cahokia and Pueblo Bonita, engineered profound changes to the world around them. Everywhere that Indians lived, landscapes bore the imprint of human activity. Fire was a particularly important means of improvement for those who hunted. Although such people did not turn forests into fields, they did burn woodlands to make meadows or clear underbrush, the better to attract and the easier to kill game.

Lack of agriculture did not always correlate with lower population density. In the centuries before Europeans arrived in the Americas, California's population probably topped three hundred thousand. Then, as now, most of its inhabitants lived close to the coast or in nearby interior valleys. The higher density of population in these parts was not a result of agricultural surpluses; farming made almost no inroads into precolonial California, whose inhabitants hunted, fished, and gathered. These activities sustained a relatively large total population, thanks to a wealth of resources and to the ingenuity with which natives adapted to and altered local ecosystems.

In California and across North America, political and linguistic diversity went hand in hand. The primacy of local control and the absence of centralized states with administrative agents worked against the development of common tongues. The lack of written languages in North America also stood in the way of any standardizing tendencies.

It is easy to overstate the degree to which these unifying and standardizing trends had triumphed on the other side of the north Atlantic. One thousand years ago, or for that matter five hundred years ago, most Europeans could not read or write, and they spoke a local language that seemed at best a very distant cousin to the ones used at court in London, Paris, Madrid, or other capitals. Still, Latin provided a common tongue for Europe's literate minority, and the promotion of the "King's English" in England (and its equivalent in other European monarchies) gave Europeans far more linguistic unity than had developed in North America. Likewise, the consolidation of monarchies was a work in progress in Europe, still challenged by jealous nobles and the presumptive royalty of smaller states that were being swallowed up. Again, however, the consolidation of larger kingdoms and the creation of centralized administrative structures and standing armies went well beyond anything in North America.

The mobility of Indians introduces another wedge between the worlds on one side of the Atlantic and those on the other. European peasants were often bound to the piece of land they worked, while Indian farmers relocated their fields and villages occasionally and always spent a portion of the year away hunting. The circuits of Indians who did not farm were even longer and wider. By contrast, various laws prohibited European commoners from hunting at all; this was a right reserved for nobles. For meat and animal power, Europeans depended instead on livestock, as the peoples of the Americas could not.

Early modern European theories of social stages have bequeathed to us the tendency to perceive these dissimilarities as evidence of European progress and Indian backwardness. The grip of these theories continues today. History books mark the maturation of European societies in the consolidation of monarchies, the creation of coercive mechanisms of authority under state control, the standardization of language, and the presence of sedentary populations. This schema becomes even more pronounced when lining up the technologies of Europeans and American Indians. Here, the Europeans' wheeled vehicles, oceangoing vessels, and metal weapons are set against their absence in the Americas. Taken this way, the different records of social and technological development get mistaken for manifestations of destiny.

This ledger offers a flawed reckoning of precolonial Indian achievements. It fails to account for the adjustments that Indians made that allowed them to persevere when the climate shifted. Great centers like Cahokia and Chaco Canyon were lost, and peoples around North America endured hardships. Yet in the centuries before the Atlantic was crossed, Indians were generally better fed and more physically robust than Europeans. Although it was Europeans who moved across the ocean, the mobility and adaptability of Indians within the Americas protected them more successfully from devastating famines, which periodically ravaged Europe during the Little Ice Age.

This accounting of visible divergences also misleads as an explanation for what followed the European "discovery" of the Americas. Precolonial developments influenced the ways in which Indians viewed the newcomers—the ways they met, mingled with, mated with, borrowed from, traded with, raided, and fought Europeans. The Indians' experiences and memories equipped them to adapt to the unfamiliar plants, animals, tools, and weapons the Europeans brought with them. The Indians' adaptability allowed them to accommodate the even stranger rules and rites that Europeans sought to impose on their intercourse and combat. But nothing could prepare Indians for that which they could not see, which proved to be the deadly agents of conquest on which the foundations of American Wests rested.

Chapter 2
Empires and enclaves

Two hundred years after Christopher Columbus first voyaged from Europe to the Americas, a flurry of witchcraft accusations and executions shook the social order in colonial North America. One episode took place in Salem, Massachusetts, in 1692. Another occurred far to the west in Santa Fe, New Mexico. The former is much better known today, though the latter claimed many more victims. The western incident also better reflected and was more important to the broader colonial history of North America.

Columbus, we now appreciate, discovered an Old World in 1492; his arrival created a new West, at least from the perspective of Europeans. The reverberations from Columbus's voyage reached around the globe. Yet the upheaval was greatest in the Americas, where steep population declines reduced Indian numbers by more than 90 percent in the four centuries after 1492. Absent this toll, European occupation of North America could not have proceeded as it did. Over time, microbes, which were part of a broader biotic transoceanic migration, paved the way for European conquests and pushed Indian survivors to accept more of the goods and ideas imposed on them by invaders.

It is essential, however, that even very short introductions not drop the sense of "over time," not treat the demise of Indian America as wholly determined by environmental forces unleashed in Columbus's immediate wake. Control over North American lands remained hotly contested and quite uncertain for hundreds of years after 1492. Well into the eighteenth century, the vast majority of North American Indians had not become the subordinates of European colonizers. In fact, in most places there were no European settlements yet. Where there were, the security of these enclaves, like the fate of the empires that Europeans claimed to have built, rested on a variety of negotiated arrangements and cultural mixings with native peoples. And on the grasslands of the Great Plains, the spread of horses, though it was part of the process by which Afro-Eurasian plants and animals supplanted species native to the Americas, wrought a cultural revolution that enabled several Indian groups to dramatically expand their realms.

First contacts

In the first century after 1492, Europeans had trouble holding any place on the continent north of the Caribbean and of Mexico. The vessels of fishers and explorers probed the Atlantic coast, but they could not locate the passage to Asia that they sought. They did find Indians, who thwarted efforts by Europeans to found permanent colonies on the mainland and generally kept trade at the shores and on their terms. When Europeans ventured inland, their forays failed to establish lasting settlements, though what they left behind unsettled scores of Indian communities.

We know very little about the first contacts between North American Indians and Europeans and even less about what the former made of the latter. European witnesses claimed that Indians conceived the newcomers' ships as floating islands or giant monsters and worshiped their metal tools and weapons. Indians supposedly also assumed Europeans to be supernatural beings.

Whatever the first impressions, more enduring ones soon took hold. Technologies obviously mattered. Indians called Europeans by names that translated as "woodworkers," "metalworkers," "clothmakers," "axemakers," and "knifemen." Others simply designated them "strangers," indicating how quickly the newcomers lost their godly status. This name also reflects how different these bearded men looked (and how bad these infrequent bathers smelled). Strange, too, were the ways of Europeans, whose presumption of superiority and sense of entitlement made them unwelcome guests.

The estrangement complicated, but did not preclude, entanglements between Indians and Europeans. Along the Atlantic seaboard, exchanges accompanied encounters. Indians appreciated the advantages that metal tools offered and (like almost all people) attached added value to certain exotic items that were not produced locally. Yet, in the first century after 1492, Indians held important advantages in shaping barter along the coastline. Europeans needed the foods and increasingly wanted the furs that Indians provided—more than Indians needed and wanted what Europeans offered. That allowed Indians to determine the setting and duration of trading sessions. It also gave them the better of the deals, at least as they saw it. "The Beaver does everything perfectly well," an Indian informant explained to a French missionary in the early seventeenth century. "It makes kettles, hatchets, swords, [and] knives." Europeans, from this native's perspective, "have no sense," for "they give us twenty knives...for one Beaver skin."

These European goods circulated inland, following long-standing native trading routes. In these cases, no Europeans were directly involved. Indeed, European things moved far ahead of European people into the interior of North America, as did microbes, plants, and animals from the other side of the Atlantic.

Those Europeans who explored inland during the sixteenth century often traveled along those same trails, but they were less interested in establishing trade than in demanding tribute.

Consider the expeditions of Francisco Vásquez de Coronado and Hernando de Soto in the late 1530s and early 1540s. Both men had been part of earlier Spanish conquests, and they borrowed from the playbook for domination developed in the Caribbean and Mexico. Lured by tales of cities of gold, Coronado journeyed north from Mexico, using swords, firearms, horses, and war dogs to terrorize Indian villagers in what is today Arizona and New Mexico. From there the search for precious metals sent him north and east onto the Great Plains, where he found neither gold nor great cities and accumulated expedition bills that bankrupted him. De Soto's trek from Florida across what is today the southeastern United States took him into a country with bigger towns and chiefdoms, the holdovers from Mississippian cultures. De Soto, too, tried to dominate his way across these countries, and his forces did plenty of damage to the native towns they sought to subjugate. But the invaders did not emerge unscathed. De Soto himself died along the banks of the lower Mississippi River in 1542, and fewer than half of his men made it back alive to Mexico City.

The greater devastation, however, befell Indians and ensued from the germs De Soto's men brought with them. These continued to spread long after the Spaniards had departed. The trails of specific epidemics are impossible now to recover. What is clear is that the region, so densely settled when De Soto's expedition passed through it in the second quarter of the sixteenth century, had been significantly depopulated when Europeans returned in the seventeenth century. By then, many towns had disappeared, most chiefdoms had collapsed, and worlds much older than Europeans understood had been swept away.

New England and New Mexico in the seventeenth century

During the second post-Columbian century, Europeans gained a more significant foothold in North America, though their territorial assertions looked far more impressive on the maps they drew than on the ground they presumed to occupy. In a few places, particularly a narrow band along the Atlantic coast, English claims translated into actual colonies where Europeans generally came to dominate Indians. To the west, however, European settlements and settlers were fewer, and relations with Indians more complicated. The colonies that developed during the seventeenth century were diverse, and their interactions with Indians varied, as a brief comparison of two cases, Massachusetts and New Mexico, highlights.

In most American history textbooks, the beginnings of English colonization in Massachusetts date to 1620, when the Pilgrims established a settlement at Plymouth. The colonists survived their initial hardships, the familiar origin story goes, thanks to generous gifts from local Indians. But that chronology and the explanation for the first Thanksgiving ignores earlier contacts and erases the context in which Indians aided Pilgrims. Decades of dealings preceded the Pilgrims' landing in Plymouth. This locale was the territory of the Wampanoags. Like other coastal tribes, the Wampanoags welcomed foreign goods, while managing the presence of foreigners, allowing mariners onshore only for limited stays. They could not, however, contain the germs of Europeans. Beginning in 1616 and continuing for three years, invasive pathogens decimated the tribe's ranks. Their communities shattered and their security imperiled by their enemies, the Narragansetts, who had not yet suffered grievous losses, the Wampanoags allowed the English to settle. At the time, the Wampanoags' decision made sense: the tools of the Europeans had some value, and the inability of Europeans to survive without assistance suggested that the Pilgrims posed a lesser threat to the Wampanoags than did the Narragansetts.

The Wampanoags were not the only Indians in the seventeenth century to make this calculation, but they were among the first to suffer the catastrophic consequences of underestimating the destructive potency of the newcomers. For the assistance of the Wampanoags, the Pilgrims gave thanks, though not so much to the Indians as to their God for miraculously clearing the wilderness for them. Saved from starvation, the colonists at Plymouth and later around Massachusetts Bay multiplied. Pressure on Indian landholdings intensified, sparking bloody wars in the 1630s and 1670s. By the closing years of the seventeenth century, the Wampanoags, along with most of the native peoples in a region that had now been recast as a "New England," had been largely dispossessed. Their ranks greatly thinned by diseases, warfare, and migrations, the Indians who remained scraped by on the margins of colonial society. Some resided in "Praying Towns," where missionaries tutored them in the ways of Christianity and "civilization."

Developments in other English colonies resembled those in New England, but at the end of the seventeenth century the displacement of Indians and the dominion of a settler colonial society extended at most two hundred miles inland from the Atlantic coast. In the few interior spots where Europeans planted outposts, drawing colonists proved difficult, as did efforts to dictate to Indians. Even where colonizers presumed to rule, they learned the limits of their power.

That was the case in New Mexico, though the Spanish pretended their domination over Indians was as complete as that of the English in Massachusetts (or, for that matter, equivalent to that which earlier conquistadors had achieved in the Caribbean, central Mexico, and the Andes). In 1598, a little more than half a century after Coronado left, the Spanish returned to New Mexico—this time with intentions to stay and to reign. Spaniards quickly made it clear that they would tolerate no opposition. After squashing resistance at Ácoma in 1599, the Spanish commander, Juan de Oñate, decreed that all Indian men in the village over the age of twenty-five would have one foot cut off, while all over twelve would be enslaved for twenty years. On the surface, the brutal crackdown had the desired effect. Divided into dozens of separate communities (the term *pueblo* was Spanish for town and was used by Spanish colonizers to refer to town-dwelling Indians in New Mexico) that zealously guarded their autonomy, Pueblo Indians could mount no united challenge to Spanish conquest. Those at Ácoma and other towns in the region of the Rio Grande River were left with seemingly little choice but to bend to Spanish authority, forced to pay tribute in labor, crops, and sexual services. Pueblo Indians, like those in Massachusetts, appeared also to have surrendered in the spiritual contest with Catholic missionaries. Some four thousand Indians were baptized in the first decade of Spanish colonization; more than twenty thousand had converted by the mid-1620s.

Yet these numbers deceived. To the dismay of the padres, Indian converts backslid with alarming frequency. Many appeared to treat the Catholic faith and its rites as supplements, not substitutes, for indigenous beliefs and practices. Missionaries responded with harsh punishments, but whippings did not stem the persistence of traditions.

Beyond the fields of the various Pueblos, Spanish control over Indians within the expansive terrain they mapped as New Mexico was even more illusory. Without precious metals to mine or other obvious sources of wealth to harvest, New Mexico was no magnet for men on the make. Unlike Massachusetts, where a sizeable immigration of families combined with natural increases to bolster colonial ranks and tip the balance of numbers (and power) ever more against Indians, New Mexico attracted few European men and almost no European women. The lack of a large settler colonial population made it hard enough for the Spanish to keep Pueblo Indians subjugated, and these Indians lived in contained villages whose homes and fields (and food supplies) were vulnerable to attack. Other Indians within the borders of the colony, especially the Navajos and Apaches, were less sedentary. The Navajos and Apaches were themselves relatively recent arrivals to the region, having migrated from points north and west a few centuries earlier. Since their relocation, Navajos and Apaches had traded with Pueblo peoples, though at times they had raided to get what they wanted. The entrance of the Spanish disrupted these patterns. Spanish levies on Pueblo supplies deprived them of the surplus harvests they had previously been able to exchange with Navajos and Apaches. So the Navajos and Apaches shifted increasingly to raiding. This they could do more successfully thanks to their acquisition of horses (which the Spanish had introduced into the Americas). These raids, in turn, made the Pueblos more dependent on the Spanish for protection. And the failure of the Spanish to defend them emboldened raiders and created greater opposition to colonial rule among the Pueblos.

All of this made the revolt that erupted in 1680 both predictable and unexpected. It was predictable that unrest would trigger some kind of uprising. For decades, religious repression, economic oppression, and sexual exploitation of women had generated discontent among the Pueblos and sparked periodic flare-ups of local, anticolonial fervor. In the 1670s, the burdens of increased raiding and the onset of drought, which further diminished the aura of Spanish protectors, made the situation more combustible. It was no surprise, then, that in 1673 inhabitants at Tewa Pueblo demonstrated their defiance by publicly performing traditional dances. The Spanish responded in their usual way. They arrested and tortured forty-seven Tewas, from whom they extracted confessions of practicing "sorcery"—the Spaniards' interpretation of Indian efforts to invoke supernatural powers. Three of the convicted were hanged, and a fourth committed suicide; others were whipped and sold into slavery. What was unprecedented was the extent to which Indians from so many different Pueblos joined together seven years later. Crucial to the creation of this united front was Popé, a man who had been among those flogged at Tewa in 1673 and who took the lead in plotting a coordinated attack

22

against the Spanish. When it came on August 10, 1680, it caught the Spanish almost completely unawares and sent survivors fleeing southward.

During the revolt and its immediate aftermath, anticolonial fury targeted particularly the manifestations of Catholicism. Numerous priests were slain, churches burned, and images of saints smeared with excrement. Indians who had converted to Christianity plunged into water to cleanse themselves of their previous baptisms. This was part of a broader movement to revitalize native traditions by renouncing ties to Spanish things and Spanish thinking.

But the restoration of precolonial ways was never complete, and the spirit of unity did not endure. Freed from colonial domination, many Indians wished to keep the tools, crops, and livestock that they had adapted. Others turned against Popé's leadership, which was at odds with traditions of local autonomy. When neither raids nor drought relented, the fractures deepened—and opened the path for Spanish reconquest in 1692.

On their return, the Spanish initially resorted to retribution. In 1692, the same year that nineteen convicted witches were hanged in Salem, Massachusetts, more than three times that number of Indians were executed for sorcery and sedition in Santa Fe, New Mexico.

In the following decades, however, the Spanish adopted a softer stance toward the Pueblos. Not wanting to stir another Indian rebellion, Spanish authorities showed more tolerance for indigenous practices and reduced their economic demands on Pueblo communities. Through the eighteenth century in New Mexico and beyond, Spanish officials looked for alternative models by which to maintain and expand their place in North America.

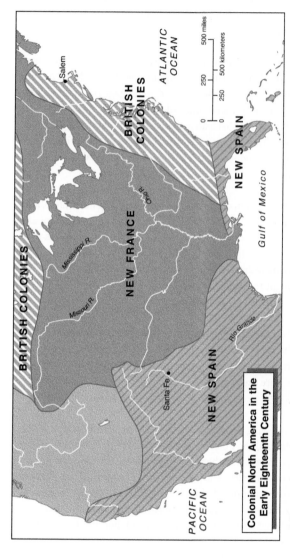

1. Like many maps that delineate territories in colonial America, this one treats the claims of European powers as if they represented the situation on the ground in the seventeenth and eighteenth centuries. These maps are still used today, even though they distort the history.

Alternatives

Alternatives abounded in the vast country between New Mexico and New England. In the first half of the eighteenth century, France claimed much of the territory between the supposed English and Spanish realms. It was, however, home to few French. Unable to dominate natives militarily and dependent on them economically, French colonists and colonial officials learned to accommodate Indian ways. The slippery common grounds that French and Indians created together in the interior of North America included an array of cultural fusions and a variety of political, economic, and religious arrangements. And in the middle of the continent, some Indians asserted their dominance by overrunning the claims of other Indians and eclipsing the imperial designs of Europeans.

The French did not initially intend to be cocreators of such alternatives, but the policies of the French state and the conditions and cultures they encountered in North America pushed their colonial regime away from the models of occupation and domination constructed by the English and the Spanish. Like their imperial rivals, the first French explorers sought a path to riches, preferably by finding a passage through North America to Asia. Failing that, men on the make hoped to exploit the resources and peoples of North America, while men on a mission aimed to save the souls of Indians. To these ends, the French established Québec in 1608. From there, Frenchmen made their way up the St. Lawrence River and into a network of inland waterways. None, however, led across the continent. Nor did the dense forests that surrounded the rivers and lakes of northeastern North America bear any signs of gold or silver, and the short growing season limited the region's agricultural potential. All this dampened any ardor for permanent relocation from France to New France, which the French monarchy did little to encourage. By the middle of the seventeenth century, fewer than two thousand French colonists, almost all men, inhabited New France,

a census that was one-twentieth the settler population in
neighboring New England.

Among them, and often well ahead of most in bringing a French
presence deeper into the interior of North America, was a
determined cadre of Catholic priests. As in New Mexico and
Massachusetts, missionaries in New France aimed to convert
Indians to Christianity. Saving Indians meant they must give
up most of their customary practices, beginning with what
missionaries identified as the natives' licentious sexuality. Still,
French missionaries showed greater tolerance for the persistence
of some traditions than did their Spanish or English counterparts.
They also prepared themselves far better to live among Indians,
learning specific native languages and gaining a degree of
familiarity with native customs before commencing their work
among Indians. Unlike Spanish and English missionaries, French
priests needed those skills because they set up their outposts in
Indian villages far beyond the realm of French control.

Along with missionaries, traders led the French advance. Their
pursuit of animal skins, especially beaver pelts, required that they,
too, develop greater understanding of Indian ways and come to
better understandings with them. Although French authorities
tried to keep colonists laboring in the fields that stretched along
the St. Lawrence River, the lure of the forests was too great.
Running into the woods (hence the name *coureurs de bois*)
without official sanction, traders moved into the Great Lakes
region and later into the Mississippi Valley. But this expansion did
not displace Indians. To the contrary, the French lacked the
numbers to impose their will on Indians. Besides, the venture that
brought traders into the continent's interior depended on the
continued presence and participation of Indians. It was Indian
men who hunted and trapped the animals and Indian women who
prepared the skins. To secure the cooperation of Indian partners,
French traders adjusted their expectations about prices and
commerce and respected the different protocols of reciprocity and

gift-giving that governed exchanges in woodland Indian societies. To create ties to Indian communities and to provide themselves with essential partners, *coureurs de bois* married Indian women. What emerged was a world of mixed ways and mixed-race offspring, which facilitated trade but concerned colonial officials. From their standpoint, the blendings threatened to turn fur traders into cultural traitors, into "white Indians."

Yet French authorities made many concessions of their own to Indians. In need of allies against their more populous English adversaries, French officials had good reason to bridge cultural differences and make common cause with Indians, especially with Algonquian speakers in the Great Lakes region. Having suffered at the hands of the Iroquois, the Algonquians were equally in need and welcomed the protection of the French "father." But though the French referred to Indians as "children," the relationship between French fathers and Indian children was quite different from the patriarchal norms of European families (and societies). While Indians expected protection and provision from a father, these did not translate as they did in Europe to the right to discipline or the power to dominate. The alliance that French and Algonquians fashioned remained a delicate arrangement, whose maintenance required that rituals of conciliation be repeatedly performed and useful misunderstandings go unchallenged.

That Algonquians accepted the French both as "fathers" and as husbands did not indicate their subordination, but over time, trade and both human and ecological imperialism created among them a growing dependency on European goods and a weakening of their position. The beaver could do "everything perfectly well" as long as there were lots of beavers and the Indians' demand for European things was limited. But as French and English traders introduced guns into the exchange networks, they initiated an arms race among Indians. To get more guns, Indians had to collect more skins, which resulted in the depletion of beavers in heavily trapped areas. That, in turn, pushed Indians to expand their hunting/

trapping zones, which heightened conflicts between groups. Alcohol, too, became a potent weapon for Europeans. It further tipped the balance of trading power by giving Europeans a commodity that Indians wanted badly enough to undermine long-standing understandings of the relationship between humans and animals and to overwhelm strictures against overhunting.

Taken together, guns, alcohol, and especially germs changed the means and ends of warfare. Where earlier combat among woodland Indians had emphasized captive-taking and honor-making, the so-called Beaver Wars of the seventeenth century showed that Indians, in this case the Iroquois, now looked to take over territories, even at the cost of higher casualties. The Iroquois emerged in the short term as the winners in the Beaver Wars; their invasions scattered Algonquians, driving them to the west and into alliance with the French. In the longer run, as became apparent in the first half of the eighteenth century, both Iroquois and Algonquians, along with many other woodland Indians, were losing ground to Europeans in eastern North America.

To the west, some Indian peoples were also losing ground to newcomers, but on the Great Plains in the eighteenth century, the winners were other Indians. On the northern plains, the Sioux (as their enemies called them), who had migrated westward onto the grasslands, emerged as the most successful expansionists. Coming eastward, the Comanches reigned across a vast swath of the southern plains. These and other invaders displaced existing indigenous societies from some lands, added to their ranks by capturing and often enslaving large numbers of people, especially females, and enriched themselves by their raiding and through their control over trading. The effective realm of "Comanchería" included territory that the Spanish mapped as theirs and extended not only over other Indians in the area but also over Spaniards. This was especially true of the new colony that the Spanish tried to plant in Texas. Comanche bands plundered older settlements in New Mexico and northern Mexico as well.

There was considerable irony in this imperial inversion. The Spanish, after all, had brought horses to the Americas. These animals abetted their conquest of native societies. But the acquisition of horses revolutionized Indian life, empowered the expansions that took place on the Great Plains, and made Indians much more formidable foes. Recognizing the importance of horses, the Spanish had tried and failed to keep them out of Indian hands. Once introduced into Indian circuits, the animals dispersed and flourished on the grasses of the Plains. So did those Indians who had greatest access to horses and most decisively adapted to equestrianism. On horseback, Indians could kill bison much more effectively, which encouraged some groups to forsake farming for hunting and other groups, like the Sioux and Comanches, to move onto the Plains and move around them in pursuit of buffalo. On horseback, Indians also gained military superiority over more sedentary peoples.

Within horse cultures, new inequalities materialized. The gains of nomadic equestrians often came at the expense of those who remained wedded to a mixture of horticulture and hunting. More successful raiders and hunters not only earned greater honor but also acquired more horses—and with more horses usually came higher status and more wives. The status of women generally declined in this transition from horticultural to hunting societies. Their burdens, however, did not, as there were now more buffalo waiting to be turned by women into the products that sustained Plains Indian life.

Two hundred fifty years after Columbus bumped into the Bahamas, Europeans claimed to have carved up most of North America. That is how it appeared on the maps that Europeans made, which assigned most of the continent to one or another of their empires, a view that continues to hold sway in the geographic depictions that accompany recent editions of American history textbooks. Colonial control did, indeed, characterize Salem, Massachusetts, in the late seventeenth and early eighteenth centuries. But it was not how the situation looked in Santa Fe, New Mexico, or in almost all of the lands between Salem and Santa Fe. Then and now, our colonial maps deceive us by erasing the presence and diminishing the power of Indians. Better maps, and better histories, depict the array of Indian-European interactions on the continent—and heed not only the contractions but also the expansions of Indian countries.

Chapter 3
Making the first American West

Three hundred years after Columbus's discovery, a new nation, the United States, had recently gained its independence, but its prospects, particularly for expansion across the North American continent, did not look promising. True, the treaty that had granted the United States its independence had deeded it a vast territory from the Atlantic coast to the Mississippi River. Beyond the Appalachian Mountains stretched the "First West" of the United States. Yet this West, like so many colonial claims, was initially more a projection than a reality. Its fictional status became harder to deny after a confederation of Ohio Indians routed armies of the United States, first in 1790 and then even more decisively in 1791. In the wake of the second defeat, American diplomats tried in 1793 to purchase a piece of the West from its Indian claimants. That bid was categorically rejected. "Money to us is of no value," a leader of the Indian confederacy lectured, "and no consideration whatever can induce us to sell the lands on which we get sustenance for our women and children." For the moment, the United States lacked the unity or the power to make this West entirely its own, to make it truly an American West.

In the decades before and after the Revolution, what Americans mapped as their West remained the focus of intense rivalries between French, Spanish, and British empire-builders. Their expansionist schemes were entangled with the counter-colonial aspirations and determined occupations of diverse Indian inhabitants. Native resistance took a variety of paths, each of which proved successful for a time. But in the wake of the Louisiana Purchase, which gave the United States a farther West, and the War of 1812, which brought a further withdrawal of imperial rivals, Indians' options narrowed. By the 1820s, the inclusive relations that had characterized the lands between the Appalachians and the Mississippi had largely given way to exclusive American occupations.

Imperial rivalries

In the third quarter of the eighteenth century, the Ohio Valley emerged as the focal point of imperial competition in North America. There, in the middle of the 1750s, began a war whose battlefields spread across oceans and into Europe and Asia. In the wake of this world war, imperial mapmakers redrew boundaries across North America. France surrendered its holdings on the North American mainland; England and Spain acquired vast new claims to respective "Wests" and "Norths." During the 1760s, within the territory transferred from France to Britain, Indians launched an insurgency that showed the limits of colonial authority in the "western country." By the middle of the 1770s, the fragile political and economic détente that had been worked out between British officials and native leaders came under renewed pressure as an increasing flow of colonists from east of the Appalachians breached the borders of Indian countries to the west of the mountains.

Americans remember the global struggle of the 1750s as the "French and Indian War"; elsewhere it is referred to as the "Seven Years' War." Both names are misleading. The American designation implies that all Indians sided with the French and that French and Indian interests exactly coincided. "Seven Years' War" suggests a conflict of that duration. In fact, Indians fought on both sides and for their own reasons, and their war for control of the Ohio Valley and Great Lakes continued, on and off, for sixty years.

In the Ohio Valley, many Indians, especially those who had migrated from Pennsylvania, shared the French fear of British expansion. At the same time, they resented French attempts to monopolize trade. In addition, British leaders worked to win over natives by promising to create a fixed boundary between colonial settlements and Indian lands. Whether aligned with the French or the British, Indians fought (or chose not to fight) for their own interests, which were best served not by total victory of one or the other colonial regime but by a stalemate between imperial rivals and continuing competition between their traders.

Unfortunately for the Indians, the war dealt the French out of North America. By the 1763 Treaty of Paris, Britain gained control of Canada and of French claims below the Great Lakes and east of the Mississippi River (with the exception of New Orleans, which was transferred to Spain along with French possessions west of the Mississippi). Flush with victory and freed of competition with the French, British officials hatched plans to erect a much less accommodating regime. The British commander, Lord Jeffery Amherst, did not propose to negotiate with defeated peoples; he intended to dictate the terms of intercultural relations. The practice of making presents to Indians, which Amherst viewed as "bribes," was to be eliminated. Henceforth, British traders would pay market prices for the pelts they obtained, and misbehaving natives would be punished by cutting off their access to imported goods.

Incensed Indian war parties from dozens of villages around the Great Lakes and Ohio Valley attacked British posts in the western country and raided settlements on the eastern side of the Appalachians. British authorities saw in these attacks evidence of a vast conspiracy, but the Indians' uprising was not the work of a centrally coordinated confederation. The insurgents did, however, draw inspiration from a number of prophets, who offered similar visions of Indian renaissance through rituals of cultural purification.

The message of Indian revitalization through de-Europeanization resonated with tremendous force, but, as with the revolt staged by Pueblo Indians eighty years earlier, a complete detachment was impractical, if not unimaginable. Generations of cross-cultural exchange had woven items and ideas of European origin into the fabric of woodland Indian life. The Indians' incorporation of foreign elements included not only the adaptation of colonial things and colonial thinking but also the adoption of colonists. From their raids against backcountry settlements, Ohio Valley Indians brought back scores of captives, who, in keeping with long-standing practices, were sometimes adopted. Not all of the adopted adapted to Indian life successfully. Enough did that when the British demanded the return of prisoners as a condition of restoring peace and trade, a significant portion resisted repatriation.

Although the British put down the Indians' insurgency, the cost of fighting and the loss of fur trade revenues prompted a reversal of Amherst's vindictive policies. British officials embraced a more accommodating stance. Like the French, they acceded to certain Indian protocols. Gift-giving came back as the basis of trade, and with a royal proclamation in 1763, British leaders promised to prevent settlers from trespassing across the Appalachians.

Did the king really intend to ban colonization of the western country? Not according to George Washington, who saw the proclamation's boundary as but "a temporary expedient." Speculators on both sides of the Atlantic had schemed for decades about acquiring vast tracts of trans-Appalachian land; many anticipated an unprecedented windfall once the Crown approved enormous grants to the wealthy and well-connected. Gentlemen who missed the "present opportunity of hunting out good lands," warned Washington, "will never regain it."

The Proclamation Line also displeased humbler backcountry settlers, who harbored land acquisition dreams of their own and were contemptuous of imperial officials and their injunctions. During the 1760s, hundreds of squatters pushed into Appalachian valleys. Poaching and penetrating even deeper into Indian country were scores of white hunters, who began to make regular fall and winter hunts in what are now Kentucky and Tennessee. These "long hunters" challenged the monopoly that Indian hunters had previously held as suppliers of skins and furs. Worse still from the perspective of Ohio Valley Indians, many long hunters engaged in land hunting on the side, scouting tracts for future settlements for themselves or sometimes for wealthy speculators.

Colonial authorities could do little in the face of long hunters' brazen defiance; they had neither the money nor the manpower to police thousands of square miles of Appalachian frontier. The problem, it seemed to many gentry authorities, was that backcountry settlers in general and long hunters in particular too closely resembled the Indian peoples whose lands they invaded and whose role in the fur trade they usurped. Residents of western Pennsylvania, reported Thomas Gage, the British military commander for North America in 1772, "differ[ed] little from Indians in their manner of life."

Admitting that backcountry people "are not to be confined by any boundaries or limits," Sir William Johnson attempted to defuse conflict by convincing Indians to withdraw from contested territory. At Fort Stanwix in November 1768, he persuaded an assembly of more than three thousand Indians, principally members of the Iroquois Confederacy, to cede their claims to lands south of the Ohio River and east of the mouth of the Kanawha River. Almost completely absent from the conclave were representatives of the Shawnees and Delawares, whose villages lay closest to the lands in question and whose councils deliberated taking up arms against the British.

War came in 1774 after a group of backcountry ruffians murdered thirteen Shawnee and Mingo Indians that spring. As was customary, relatives of the victims demanded revenge. Retaliation soon escalated. Matters came to a head in October, when Virginia militiamen defeated Shawnee warriors at the Battle of Point Pleasant.

In the treaty conference that followed, Shawnee headmen yielded hunting rights south of the Ohio River but were guaranteed that the waterway would now serve as a firm boundary between Indian country and British settlements. Sensing that this line, too, would not last long, hundreds of Shawnees embarked on another westward migration. This one took them across the Mississippi River into territory that France had ceded to Spain in 1763. West of what was now Britain's "western country," they sought a new and more permanent refuge.

As the third quarter of the eighteenth century drew to a close, Spain had not yet established much of a presence on the lands it had gained from France. On paper, Spain had dramatically expanded its holdings in North America during the 1760s and 1770s. In addition to acquiring France's claims on the west side of the Mississippi River, Spain had planted a few missions in California. But across the Spanish "North," older colonies in Arizona, New Mexico, Texas, and Florida were sparsely colonized, and the islands of Spanish settlement remained surrounded by oceans of Indian countries. In Spain's newly acquired Louisiana colony, only a handful of Spanish officials actually inhabited the former French possession, and these authorities made no attempt to Hispanicize the customs, manners, or language of *habitants*. For most French colonists, the change in colonial regimes made little difference. For many Indians as well, life went on as before. Just as the British in the 1760s learned to emulate French accommodations, so, too, the Spanish in the Mississippi Valley assured Indians that trade would be encouraged and gifts would be given. Such promises attracted Shawnee migrants and inspired hope among natives who stayed east of the Mississippi that Anglo-Spanish competition might prevent a mixed but primarily still Indian country from becoming a mere western country.

The American Revolution and its aftermath

During the final quarter of the eighteenth century, Indians vigorously contested the redefinition of lands between the Appalachians and the Mississippi as a western country. As in the past, they followed a variety of strategies, including migrations, accommodations, incorporations, revitalizations, and confederations. They did so, however, in a geopolitical context that was dramatically transformed by the American Revolution. The war and resulting American independence reshuffled relations across North America, especially in the fervently disputed country between the Appalachians and the Mississippi. Into the 1790s, the disposition of these lands remained unsettled.

The sustained colonization of trans-Appalachia coincided with the beginning of the Revolutionary War. In the same month that Massachusetts minutemen engaged British soldiers at Lexington and Concord, Daniel Boone led thirty men to the Kentucky River. The Transylvania Company, the partnership of North Carolina speculators for whom Boone worked, had acquired their claim to hundreds of thousands of acres of Kentucky lands through a purchase from the Cherokees. News of that purchase disturbed rival speculators who feared being shut out. "There is something in that affair which I neither understand, nor like, and wish I may not have cause to dislike it worse as the mystery unfolds," wrote George Washington. With their own plans for engrossing Kentucky threatened, colonial governors in Virginia and North Carolina also condemned the illegal purchase and settlement made by the Transylvania Company. The call to command the

Continental Army soon diverted Washington's attentions, and the outbreak of revolution unseated the colonial governors of Virginia and North Carolina, who had voided the claims of the Transylvania Company. Still, the Transylvania enterprise had plenty of enemies among patriot elites, and among other parties of trans-Appalachian pioneers as well.

As before the Revolution, Indians divided about the best means to protect the integrity of their countries and their cultures. Among Cherokees, the decision to sell hunting lands to the Transylvania partners aggravated those divisions. In general, older headmen saw the deal as an unwelcome necessity. Younger men accused these leaders of betraying their people. Two years later, after accommodation-minded leaders agreed to cede additional lands to the revolutionary governments of Georgia, South Carolina, North Carolina, and Virginia, militants moved out, establishing new towns further west. From this new location, which afforded better access to British supplies, these secessionists vowed to fight pioneer expansion.

Similar generational and strategic splits afflicted Indian villages north of the Ohio River. Advocates of accommodation wished to remain neutral in the war between Britain and some of her colonists. If necessary they were willing to concede Kentucky to settlers but wished to see the Ohio River accepted as a permanent boundary. More militant factions rekindled the idea of a pan-Indian alliance. They also rallied to the British cause.

Or, more accurately, they rallied to their own cause with British supplies. The Indians' unwillingness to act as mere surrogates, to follow the orders of British officers and prosecute the war as the British desired, created fractures in the alliance. So did the failings of the British to provide essential supplies and gifts. Some warriors talked of severing their ties with the British and aligning with the Americans. Yet Americans repeatedly undermined these efforts by launching indiscriminate raids that killed Indians regardless of their political allegiances. Dissatisfied with the British and at odds with the Americans, many Ohio Indians joined the Delaware headman Captain Pipe in wishing openly for the return of the French. We have "never known of any other Father," Pipe told British officials, whom he downgraded as mere "brothers." In fact, though, what Ohio Indians wanted was not to exchange the French for the British but to restore an imperial competition that prevented any European empire from asserting dominance.

During the Revolution, Indians had failed to dislodge pioneers from their trans-Appalachian settlements, but they had not lost ground either. Through seven years of bloody raids and retaliations, they inflicted heavy casualties on Kentucky settlers—far higher per capita than those suffered by Americans east of the Appalachians. Nonetheless, when the terms of the peace between Great Britain and the United States reached the western country, Indians discovered to their dismay that all of the lands below the Great Lakes had been ceded to the new nation. By the 1783 Treaty of Paris, some 230 million acres of trans-Appalachian lands, all of which had supposedly been permanently guaranteed to Indians by royal decree, had now become the First West of the United States.

Of course, the remapping stipulated by the 1783 Treaty of Paris did not really alter the situation on the ground. As had been the case twenty years earlier, when a previous agreement in Paris had attached the western country to the British Empire, the 1783 accord could not alone make the West American. Just as British officers pretended that western Indians had surrendered along with the French, so Americans prepared to dictate to, not negotiate with, those whom they dismissed as defeated peoples. Indians, needless to say, did not consider themselves conquered in the 1760s or the 1780s. True, in the 1780s more than a thousand Shawnees and Delawares joined several hundred Cherokees in relocating to Spanish territory across the Mississippi. There they reunited with earlier migrants. Those who stayed behind resigned themselves to the loss of Kentucky, but a growing majority determined to contest any American occupations on the north side of the river. For ten years after the end of the Revolution, their confederated resistance effectively limited the advance of American colonization north of the Ohio River and frustrated the efforts of the national government of the United States to consolidate its control over the "Northwest Territory."

Various factors contributed to the good fortunes of the Indian confederacy. First, the British betrayal was not as complete as the latest Treaty of Paris suggested. Making peace did not mean that King George III and his ministers had reconciled themselves to the loss of the American colonies. Because the Crown's agents viewed western Indians as crucial to recovering His Majesty's possessions, they rushed to reassure their wartime partners that the alliance continued. Reneging on the treaty provision that stipulated the evacuation of British posts south of the Great Lakes, British officials promised Indians that these forts would be maintained and would dispense the gifts, trade goods, and arms that natives needed to defend their homelands. To further weaken the hold of the United States over its West, Britain returned west Florida to its Spanish enemy. This put Spain in control of the Gulf Coast and the mouth of the Mississippi. It left the western country isolated by mountains on the east and bordered by imperial rivals on the north, west, and south. For Indians, it meant that many still enjoyed the advantages of being in between.

The arrogance, incompetence, and divisions among American adversaries bolstered the Indian confederacy, too. By treating natives as conquered peoples, by allowing murderers of Indians to go unpunished, and by failing to keep squatters from trespassing across the Ohio, Americans left Indians with little choice but to unite and fight. By contrast, the new nation lacked such common purpose or concerted power. Its own confederation of states assigned the national government too few resources to quell Indian resistance or assert control over the settlement of western lands. The ratification of a national constitution strengthened the federal government, but the army of the United States initially proved unable to break Indian defiance. Convinced of their military and spiritual superiority, Indian negotiators not only rebuffed the American bid to buy lands but also insisted that the United States remove all the trespassers from the territory north of the Ohio River.

Recognizing the growing discontent of western Americans with a national government that could not defeat Indians and would not offer land to would-be settlers on sufficiently generous terms, both the Spanish and the British attempted to detach westerners (and the western country) from the United States. To that end, Spanish and British officials entered into not very secret talks with western leaders and introduced attractive land policies. For the Spanish, this resulted during the 1790s in the resettlement of several hundred Kentuckians and Tennesseans, including Daniel Boone, in the Louisiana colony. For the British, the promise of nearly free land and almost no taxation, if not parliamentary representation, persuaded similar numbers from New England and New York to relocate in Upper Canada (Ontario).

Yet the United States possessed a great and growing advantage over its imperial rivals and its Indian antagonists: numbers. In the 1790s, the American population topped four million, having doubled every twenty-five years during the eighteenth century. The trans-Appalachian segment was expanding even more quickly. By 1790, the first national census registered more than seventy thousand people in Kentucky, with another thirty thousand scattered in other western country settlements. By comparison, the population of Indians north of the Ohio River numbered only about twenty thousand, and this figure was declining as a result of wars, diseases, and migrations.

In 1794, the United States sent another army to crack the power and unity of the Indian confederacy. Its commander, General

Anthony Wayne, proved much abler than his predecessors. At Fallen Timbers in what is now northwestern Ohio, Wayne's troops defeated the Indian forces. It was an important triumph, though it alone was not decisive. What turned Fallen Timbers into a catastrophic defeat for confederated Indians were changes in the international scene. Locked in conflict with revolutionary France, the monarchies of Spain and Britain decided to avoid a confrontation with the American republic. Consequently, the Spanish temporarily opened the Mississippi to American navigation, and the British betrayed their Indian allies once more. They closed their forts to retreating Indians and cut them off from resupply. Without this assistance, Indians could not stop Wayne from systematically destroying villages and burning cornfields. Surviving warriors scattered back to defend their homes. At the treaty session that followed, Indians surrendered much of what soon became the state of Ohio.

The Jeffersonian persuasion

Fallen Timbers marked a critical turning point. Never again would Indians in the trans-Appalachian West, or for that matter in subsequent Wests, contest American conquest from so favorable a position. In the first quarter of the nineteenth century, Indians resisted in familiar ways, but widening disparities in numbers and technology diminished their chances for all but the most ephemeral successes in what was ever more clearly an American West. That England, France, and Spain largely withdrew from competing with the United States also tilted the balance of power further away from the Indians, who had previously been able to play these imperial rivals off against each another.

The election of Thomas Jefferson to the presidency in 1800 and the control Jeffersonians assumed over the national government for the next generation contributed as well to the more rapid colonization of western lands and the speedier dispossession of Indian peoples. In contrast to the restraints that George

Washington and like-minded Federalists sought to impose on western settlement, Jefferson insisted that "those who labour in the earth are the chosen people of God" and that agrarian expansion was the key to preserving the virtue of the American republic. For Jefferson and his followers, that conviction translated into laws that reduced the price and eased the terms of sale for public lands. As Jefferson hoped, these policies enabled more white men to acquire lands and tested Indians' control over their holdings. While Jefferson professed faith that Indians could be incorporated into the United States, he also pressed them to cede their "surplus" lands and exchange their current territories for lands to the west. That possibility became more plausible with the completion of the Louisiana Purchase in 1803.

The Purchase itself was rather improbable. In the year of Jefferson's election, Spain's retrocession of the Louisiana Territory to France reestablished a French imperial presence in North America. Napoleon aimed to reclaim France's former domain, a move that would have halted and perhaps even rolled back American expansion. Napoleon's plans were altered, however, when his army was unable to subdue rebellious slaves in Saint-Domingue, soon to be renamed Haiti. Napoleon's agents then surprised their American counterparts, who were negotiating only for New Orleans, with an offer to sell all of the Louisiana Territory. Although Jefferson worried about the constitutionality of the deal, pragmatism in pursuit of land led him to embrace the acquisition of Louisiana. The transfer, which at a cost of $15 million nearly doubled the territory of the United States, opened what Jefferson prophesied would be an "empire for liberty." The purchase also cleared imperial competitors from the western borders of the first American West and deprived trans-Appalachian Indians of assistance from what was now the new West of the United States.

Within the First West, though, the British still meddled from Canada. American officials and settlers in the First West were quick to blame the British for all troubles with Indians south of

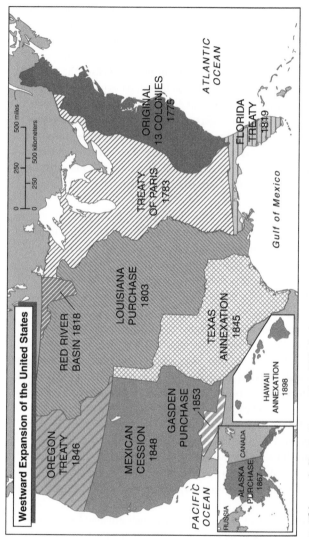

Westward Expansion of the United States

ATLANTIC OCEAN

ORIGINAL 13 COLONIES 1775

FLORIDA TREATY 1819

Gulf of Mexico

TREATY OF PARIS 1783

RED RIVER BASIN 1818

LOUISIANA PURCHASE 1803

TEXAS ANNEXATION 1845

OREGON TREATY 1846

MEXICAN CESSION 1848

GASDEN PURCHASE 1853

HAWAII ANNEXATION 1898

PACIFIC OCEAN

RUSSIA   ALASKA PURCHASE 1867   CANADA

500 miles
0   250   500 kilometers
0   250   500

2. This map indicates the years in which the American nation acquired new territories. It does not, however, reflect the ways in which the new borders remained contested.

the Great Lakes. That made western representatives particularly ready for another round of combat with Britain.

When that war came in 1812, its outbreak raised Indian hopes anew. Once more British supplies flowed to Indian allies. Once more a confederation of Indians from diverse tribes gathered to halt American expansion. But war's end brought yet another betrayal by the British and, this time, fatally broke the possibilities of an Indian confederacy east of the Mississippi. After 1815, the British stopped encouraging and supplying Indians south of the Great Lakes. Spain, its empire crumbling at home and abroad, also pulled back, ceding Florida in 1819 to the American republic.

By 1820, the northern, southern, and western borders of the first American West had been secured. Inside the region, Indians found themselves ever more encircled by multiplying numbers of American settlers. No longer able to mount effective military resistance, most Indians in the territory north of the Ohio River were pushed out to lands west of the Mississippi in the decade after the War of 1812. South of Kentucky, more Indians hung on, but their future was increasingly jeopardized by a flood of white Americans, joined by their African-American slaves (approximately one million of whom were forcibly moved into the First West during the first half of the nineteenth century). This great migration of free and unfree laborers soon transformed the southern portions of this West into the "Cotton Kingdom." In this empire for the liberty of slaveholders, the fate of Indians still resident rested increasingly on the purported mercy of the government of the United States.

Chapter 4
Taking the farther West

The governor of a border state warned about the dangers of "hordes" of unwelcome immigrants "whose progress we cannot arrest." Although his nation had once encouraged immigration from its neighbor, recent history had taught the governor that they were a destabilizing presence. Rather than embracing the culture of their new country, these immigrants refused to assimilate, continuing to speak in their native tongue and maintaining their attachments to their former nation. Unless their incursions were halted, the foreigners would soon outnumber and overwhelm the citizens of this border state.

The governor's fears may sound familiar, but in this case the year was 1845. The state was California, though it was then part of Mexico. The unsanctioned immigrants about whom Governor Pio Pico worried were from the United States. Pico had reason to be concerned, especially when he considered the contrasting fortunes of American and Mexican expansionism over the previous decades.

The United States had staked its claims to the country west of the Mississippi River in the first years of the nineteenth century, but initial explorations cast the region as "the Great American Desert." That characterization dampened enthusiasm for American settlement beyond the eastern fringe of the Louisiana Purchase.

Better to leave this inhospitable terrain as a reserve for fur traders and Indians, American leaders reasoned. The latter would include those ejected from the first American West, in a process then called "Indian removal," a generous euphemism for what we would today classify as "ethnic cleansing."

Yet by the time the last Indian removals from the First West were being carried out, the demands of Americans for lands farther west, within and beyond the borders of the Louisiana Purchase, were creating conflicts with existing occupants and rival claimants. Over time, these claims displaced prior arrangements between fur traders and Indians. They also led to war between the United States and Mexico and to a peace that turned what had been the Mexican North into the southwestern quadrant of the "Great West" of the United States. At the time, expansion-minded Americans justified the war and trumpeted the acquisition as the fulfillment of the nation's "manifest destiny"; American opponents of the war and Mexicans, then and now, deemed it an unjust war and immoral conquest.

Almost at the same moment that the war with Mexico ended, the discovery of gold in California precipitated an unprecedented torrent of people heading to the western end of the continent. The Gold Rush brought men (and this was a migration that was overwhelmingly male) from across the nation and around the globe to California. Its reverberations reached just as far. But its consequences were most devastating for California's native peoples. Probably no other episode in the history of the United States deserves the label "genocide" more than the extermination of California Indians.

Removals

Returning in 1806 from a two-and-a-half-year journey that had taken them from St. Louis to the mouth of the Columbia River on the Pacific coast and back, Meriwether Lewis and William Clark reported that their Corps of Discovery had fulfilled the directions given by President Thomas Jefferson. The explorers insisted that they had found, as Jefferson requested, "the most practicable and navigable passage across the continent," and they sent enthusiastic descriptions of the abundance of the countries in the newly purchased Louisiana Territory. Skeptics soon questioned the practicality of the passage that Lewis and Clark stumbled on, much of it mountainous and not navigable by water. Subsequent explorers also disputed the feasibility of the Great Plains as a place for yeoman farmers. Trained to assess the arability of land on the basis of the number and type of trees that it supported, Americans in the early nineteenth century did not believe grasslands made good farmlands. That explained why explorer Stephen Long's 1819 description of the Plains as a "Great American Desert" stuck, and why American leaders reenvisioned the region as, instead of an empire for liberty and white settlement, a refuge for Indians (and for a small number of Euro-Americans who interacted with them as traders and missionaries).

The fur trade in the Louisiana Territory was already a well-established business at the beginning of the nineteenth century. It got a boost from the observations of Lewis and Clark and from the depletion of beavers in lands to the east. Heeding Jefferson's instructions, Lewis and Clark catalogued the profusion of animals they encountered and alerted Indians to the "commercial dispositions" of the United States. Along the Missouri River, however, the Indians whom Lewis and Clark met had their own ideas about exchange and their own experience of intercourse (both sexual and economic) with French traders. In the first decades of the nineteenth century, the Americans who succeeded in the trans-Mississippi region generally emulated their French predecessors, marrying Indian women and accepting native notions about the primacy of gifts. In pursuit of skins, hundreds of Americans pushed into the Rocky Mountains and to the "Oregon Country" beyond. Many of these so-called mountain men took to trapping for themselves, taking over a role previously left for

Indians. But most mountain men recognized they worked lands that still belonged to Indians and understood as well the necessity of following the "customs of the country," particularly in establishing relationships with Indian women.

Back east, in the First West, the declining supply of beavers and the escalating demand for farmlands undermined the fur trade and traditions of cohabitation of Indians and Euro-Americans. Publicly, President Jefferson voiced support for incorporating Indians within American society, not removing them from it—though only after Indians gave up hunting and took up farming. While this prescription ignored the fact that woodland Indians already drew most of their subsistence from agriculture (albeit from crops cultivated by women, not men), it became a preferred formulation for American policy-makers and for missionaries engaged in teaching Indians the "arts of civilization."

The first decades of the nineteenth century, however, saw the political tide turn away from assimilating Indians and toward expelling them. Advocates for removing Indians contended that Indians would not or could not make the transition to "civilization," at least not speedily enough to remain within the settled boundaries of the United States. Others cited the opposition that some tribes had demonstrated during the War of 1812 as evidence of the treachery of all Indians and the need to push them west. Some maintained that these moves were for the Indians' good; only by eviction could Indians be saved from the pernicious influences of frontier society and given the space and time to adapt to a new world. Often left unspoken was the driving force behind removal: the land hunger of a rapidly growing American population.

That tide threatened to sweep aside any Indians or government officials who stood in its way. Pressure built first in the Old Northwest Territory (the lands north of the Ohio River and south of the Great Lakes). As waves of settlers flooded Indian countries north of the Ohio River in the first two decades of the nineteenth century, federal officials negotiated (or largely dictated) treaties in which Indian ceded their lands. In exchange, the removed received annuity payments and permanent new territories to the west, primarily in present-day Kansas and Nebraska.

Around the same time, similar forces were at work in that portion of the Louisiana Territory along the west bank of the Mississippi River just south of St. Louis. Here, federal authorities tried to offer Indians some protection. In 1809 Meriwether Lewis, now governor of Louisiana, issued a proclamation ordering squatters off Indian holdings. Lewis's suicide cost Indians a defender. Six years later, William Clark, as the appointed governor of the Missouri Territory, confronted the same situation. And Clark, like Lewis, declared that white trespassers must leave. But Clark had little power to enforce his edict and no means to thwart the power of voters. Almost immediately, the territorial assembly, which unlike Clark was elected by local citizens, countermanded the governor with a petition to Congress asking that Indians be relocated. When Missouri became eligible for statehood and the governorship became an elected position, Clark stood for the office. As the best known man in the territory with the most impressive resume of service, he assumed he would win. Opponents, though, ran a campaign that attacked Clark for being too accommodating to Indians. They also accused him of fathering a child by an Indian woman (which in fur-trading circles was the norm but in the new era of Missouri politics was cast as disreputable). On Election Day in 1820, Clark lost by a margin greater than two to one. Within a few years, most Indians had surrendered their lands within the state of Missouri. Ironically, it was William Clark, reassigned as a federal superintendent of Indian agencies, who negotiated many of the treaties and oversaw the removals.

The election of Andrew Jackson in 1828 put in the White House a champion of white homesteaders—and of Indian removal. During President Jackson's two terms, much of the focus turned to Indians

in the Old Southwest (now the southeastern United States),
a region where General Jackson had previously won battles
against Indians. There, the profits to be made from growing cotton
with slave labor made taking Indian landholdings ever more
compelling. As Missouri senator Thomas Hart Benton discerned,
the removal of Indians "would make room for the spread of slaves."

Yet despite Jackson's fervent support for a general removal bill, his
effort faced considerable opposition. In Congress, his political foes
fought the Removal Act. He also contended with the Supreme
Court, which issued a decision in favor of the rights of Cherokees.
The Cherokees themselves resisted their removal in Congress,
in courts, and in the court of public opinion. Appealing to
Americans' sense of justice, they touted how well they had
mastered the arts of civilization. They pointed to their success
as farmers and to their adoption of a written language and a
republican form of governance. These points won Cherokees more
sympathy, especially once the cause of antiremoval was attached
to that of antislavery (though here opponents of slavery had to
overlook the ways the Cherokees' success as farmers was owing
to their ownership of African-American slaves).

While the Cherokees and their white supporters delayed the tide,
they could not stop it. Removal legislation narrowly won passage,
leading to the forced exodus of Indians from the southeastern
United States. The Cherokees delayed their eviction, but in 1838
they followed other eastern Indians into exile. Thousands perished
on the "Trail of Tears," which took the Cherokees from Georgia,
North Carolina, and Tennessee to new homes in what is now
Oklahoma. Bitter divisions over the treaty that led to removal split
survivors, as they struggled, like other banished Indians, to adapt
to the grasslands that were so different from the woodlands they
had known.

More than a century and a half after the Trail of Tears, the United
Nations defined "ethnic cleansing" as "a purposeful policy" by

which one ethnic or religious group uses "force or intimidation to remove from a given area persons of another ethnic or religious group." The definition was adopted to describe events in Croatia and Bosnia in the early 1990s. It applies retrospectively to Indian removals in the first four decades of the nineteenth century. The many treaties that the United States reached with various Indian nations can hardly obscure the force and intimidation that purged the territory east of the Mississippi River of most of its native inhabitants.

From Mexican North to American Southwest

The events that particularly alarmed Mexican officials like Pio Pico had occurred in Texas, when the Mexican government had encouraged immigration there from the United States. Beginning in the 1820s and continuing into the 1830s, Americans, primarily from the southern United States, poured into Texas. By the mid-1830s, they outnumbered Tejanos (Texans with Mexican roots) by almost ten to one. Demanding provincial autonomy, the Americans clashed with Mexican authorities. In 1836, a rebellion commenced, and Texans won their war of secession. Nine years later, the United States annexed Texas, all of which gave Pico good reason to warn about the insurrectionary potential of immigrants from the United States and about that nation's expansionist capacities.

In retrospect, the policy of promoting American immigration into northern Mexico looks as dangerous as Pico deemed it and as counterintuitive as it has seemed to subsequent generations. Why invite Americans in if a chief goal was to keep the United States out? At the time, the policy did not appear so paradoxical. There were, in fact, encouraging precedents. Spain had attempted something similar in Louisiana in the 1790s, though that territory's transfer back to France and then to the United States had aborted that experiment. More enduring was what the British had done in Upper Canada. Americans who crossed that border proved themselves amenable to a shift in loyalties, which showed how tenuous national attachments remained in these years. From this, others could draw lessons: the keys to gaining and holding the affection of American transplants was to protect them from Indians, provide them with land on generous terms, require little from them in the way of taxes, and interfere minimally in their private pursuits.

For a variety of reasons, Mexico had trouble abiding by these guidelines. Like the United States four decades earlier, Mexico emerged in 1821 from its war of independence with its economy battered by the prolonged struggle to escape colonial rule and with its leadership divided on fundamental questions of governance and political economy. Also like the United States, the new nation's government confronted the problem of consolidating control over a vast territory much of which was Mexican in name only. The difference was that the challenges facing Mexico were greater in almost every respect. Its postwar economy was more badly damaged, and its early national political splits between "conservatives" and "liberals" ran even deeper than those between the American "Federalists" and "Democratic-Republicans." Mexico's Indians, particularly in the north, were also far more formidable. While the confederation of Ohio Indians won significant battles with American armies, its manpower was much less than that of the United States, its British backer was unreliable, and the cornfields that fed its people were readily burned. By contrast, the equestrian Indians in northern Mexico, especially the Comanches, retained advantages in numbers, remained invulnerable to attacks on their mobile food supply, and continued to launch devastating raids against sparsely populated Mexican ranches and villages.

Mexico succeeded in attracting Americans to Texas and thus added to its northern frontier population, but the government failed to win the hearts and minds of the newcomers. The inability of Mexican forces to pacify Indians stirred widespread unrest across the Mexican north (and not just among American immigrants). Mexico's economic difficulties also hampered efforts at consolidation. In addition to people, more and more goods moved from the United States into northern Mexico. Political instability further frayed the linkages between Mexico City and its more distant provinces. Unlike the United States, Mexico did not establish a clear and consistent process by which territories graduated to statehood, and more offices were subject to local elections. To the contrary, when centralizing conservatives came into power in Mexico City, they endeavored to impose greater national control, which impinged on the local liberties that Americans expected. Perhaps most upsetting to white Americans in Texas was the interference of Mexican authorities in the right to own slaves.

Texans won their freedom from Mexico and kept their slaves. Mexico did not recognize Texas's independence but did not try to reoccupy it either. Mexico's government did protest vigorously, however, when the United States annexed Texas in 1845. The quarrel became even hotter when the United States claimed that the Rio Grande formed the boundary between Texas and Mexico (as opposed to the previously recognized line at the Nueces River). When American troops entered the disputed area in 1846, Mexican forces fired on them. After what he called the shedding of "American blood on the American soil," President James K. Polk asked Congress to declare war on Mexico.

As the candidate of Andrew Jackson's Democratic Party, Polk (whose nickname, "Young Hickory," paid homage to Jackson's "Old Hickory") had campaigned for the presidency in 1844 on an ardent expansionist platform. His slogan "54-40 or fight" referred to the latitude that he insisted had to be the northwestern border between the United States and British Canada. Polk and his backers professed themselves ready to go to war with Britain to take all of the contested Oregon country. The United States, intoned the editor of a Democratic Party–aligned newspaper in

1845, had a "manifest destiny to overspread the continent allotted by Providence for the free development of our yearly multiplying millions."

Once in office, Polk compromised about the northern boundary, but his administration provoked a war about the southern one. American diplomats reached an agreement with Britain to divide the Oregon country at the 49th parallel. Polk's agents took a much harder line with Mexico, first pushing the border of Texas southward and then, after war broke out, demanding that Mexico cede a considerable portion of its domain to the United States. Although the assertion of manifest destiny that was often invoked by Polk and fellow expansionists was coined only in 1845, its claim of providential sponsorship for the expansion of the United States and the spread of American people and ideals was much older. Rationales about the right of the higher civilization to displace the lower and about bringing the blessings of Protestantism and liberty to savage heathens had been used to validate the removal of Indians. Now, under the banner of manifest destiny, many of the same rationales were deployed against Catholic Mexicans, whose religion and mixed-race heritage supposedly made them a degenerate people.

Once the American armies had conquered New Mexico and California and occupied Mexico City, talks commenced to end the war and set a new border. The most fervent American expansionists entertained the idea of incorporating all of Mexico into the United States. Mexican resistance to land cessions, domestic opposition to the absorption of millions of "mongrel" Mexicans, and the misgivings of Polk's chief negotiator ultimately resulted in a treaty that transferred "only" the northern third of Mexico to the United States. When Polk first heard this outcome, he was furious with his diplomat, Nicholas Trist. Publicly, Trist maintained that he had not been able to get more from his Mexican counterparts, whose national constitution prohibited any territorial surrender. Privately, Trist acknowledged how troubled he was by the war and his assignment: "could those Mexicans have seen into my heart at that moment, they would have known that my feeling of shame as an American was far stronger than theirs could be as Mexicans." Angry as Polk was with Trist, he recognized that reopening negotiations and reaching a new agreement would take time. That might prove costly, for sentiment against the war and against any territorial aggrandizement was growing in the United States. Like Trist, opponents alleged that the war had been started under a false pretext and that any spoils from it stained national destiny by extending not the blessings of liberty but the realm of slavery.

So Polk settled for the gains stipulated in the 1848 Treaty of Guadalupe Hidalgo. For approximately the same amount it had paid France for the Louisiana Purchase, the United States acquired a vast territory from Mexico. Its boundaries now stretched to the shores of the Pacific Ocean.

But the treaty did not bring peace to the United States, for whether that farther West would be opened or closed to slavery became the principal division between the nation's North and South. That sectional conflict escalated through the 1850s and culminated in the secession of eleven southern states, including Texas, in 1861. Four years of bloody Civil War followed before the American union was restored and the lands that had once been northern Mexico, along with the rest of the farther West, were secured for free labor.

The gold rush

On January 24, 1848, nine days before the signing of the Treaty of Guadalupe Hidalgo, gold was discovered on the property of John Sutter along the American River in California. Swarms of gold seekers overran Sutter's holdings and spread their search for nuggets to adjacent lands and rivers. Over the following months, new strikes in new streams extended the range of prospecting.

As the news circulated, it propelled people from the eastern United States, Mexico, South America, Europe, Asia, the Pacific Islands, and Australia to California. Never before in world history had so many people from so many parts assembled in one place. Conflicts often ensued from this unparalleled convergence.

Migration to the Pacific coast of North America, albeit on a much more limited scope and scale, began in the early 1840s. By 1848, a few thousand Americans, mostly from states along the Mississippi River, had trekked to the Pacific slope. Rather than repeat the route of Lewis and Clark, these overland travelers generally followed the Platte River across the Plains and then traversed the Rockies via South Pass, which was definitely more practical for wagons than the torturous path taken by Lewis and Clark's Corps of Discovery. Still, the new trail presented plenty of challenges. Unlike earlier westward migrations that typically involved moves to contiguous territories, those headed to the West Coast of North America eschewed settlement on the intervening Plains, which they viewed as inhospitable to agriculture. So instead of a short move involving a few days or weeks of travel, their journeys involved five or six months over fifteen hundred or more miles of country that Americans saw as an unfamiliar and unforgiving desert.

Although Governor Pico complained in 1845 about the influx of Americans, the vast majority of overland migrants prior to the discovery of gold did not go to California. Beginning in 1846, the first half of the trail to California filled with thousands of members of the Church of Jesus Christ of Latter-day Saints (Mormons). By moving west, they sought to protect themselves from the persecution they had suffered in Missouri and then Illinois. Stopping well short of the Pacific coast, Mormon migrants established what they hoped would be a safe refuge near the Great Salt Lake. Isolated from other Americans, they began the work of building a realm extending across the Great Basin in a territory they designated Deseret.

That isolation was short-lived, however, as thousands and then tens of thousands of overland travelers crossed the Mormons' would-be refuge on their way farther west. Old enmities often strained relations between Mormons and those headed to the Pacific slope. Blood was shed in September 1857, when a local Mormon militia along with a group of Paiute Indians massacred 120 members of a California-bound emigrant train at Mountain Meadows in southern Utah.

Before the discovery of gold in California, by far the larger number of migrants made Oregon their destination. Except for the extraordinary distances they traveled, the Oregon-bound resembled previous generations of westering pioneers. They came as families, and they came for land—to own and to farm, sufficient to support large families and to pass on to sons, who would then be able to enjoy the same "independence" as their fathers. Hopes of securing good lands ran high among men en route to the Oregon country. In their journals, they conveyed excitement about their prospects and about "seeing the elephant," the phrase that became attached to the trek that many men described as the great adventure of their lives. Women on the trail were far less exuberant. While men waxed enthusiastic with one another about hunting bison and encountering "wild Indians," women, at least in the company of other women, complained about the long days of walking and the unending toil that marked their passage across the continent. In their diaries, they also confided their reluctance about leaving homes and friends behind and questioned the decisions made for them by husbands and fathers.

The rush for gold multiplied the number of migrants and altered their destination, their composition, and their ambition. In 1849 and during the next decade, the vast majority of overland travelers went to California. The trail became much more crowded, as the hundreds or maybe thousands each year through 1848 grew to tens of thousands in 1849 and succeeding years. Women were almost entirely absent from the caravans to this new El Dorado.

"Argonauts," unlike Oregon-bound men, left families behind and dreamed not of mere independence but of riches.

Those who came by land to California were joined there by those who came by sea. From ports along the Atlantic and Gulf coasts of the United States, gold-seekers embarked on voyages that circled the tip of South America or the shorter trip to the isthmus of Central America, which required a short overland journey and then a second ship to take them on the Pacific to the port of San Francisco. At San Francisco, which mushroomed from a provincial village into a cosmopolitan metropolis, prospectors arrived from across the Atlantic and from around the Pacific. Mexicans, Chileans, French, Chinese, and Australians were especially prominent in the international cast.

Frictions arose from the start, and conflicts and discriminations intensified as competition heated. Although the earliest prospectors needed minimal tools and knowledge, this phase of California's Gold Rush was short-lived. Those who came later than 1849 often found the most easily tapped sources of gold already claimed or already exhausted. The realization that timing and luck, not labor and persistence, determined who got rich and who did not challenged traditional American ideals and added to frustrations. With more and more men digging for more elusive riches, the situation in mining areas grew more combustible. Through intimidation and violence, native-born, white Americans attempted to monopolize the gold fields for themselves. They received support from the government of the new state of California. Having bypassed the usual territorial process, California entered the union in 1850, and the American majority exerted their legislative will by enacting taxes on foreign miners. Particularly virulent animosities were directed at Chinese in California, whose antagonists pushed to close the country to additional immigration from China.

While foreigners dealt with legal and extralegal efforts aimed at their exclusion and expulsion, California's natives faced

3. Pio Pico, the last governor of Mexican California, in a family portrait. Pico, who warned of the dangers of American immigration into California, adjusted to life under U.S. rule. But many Mexicans who shared Pico's dark skin had difficulties protecting their lands and their rights under a regime that sought to deprive mixed-race individuals of the privileges of whiteness.

pronouncements and policies designed to bring about their extermination. California's Indian population had been declining for some time prior to the Gold Rush, falling from an estimated 300,000 in 1769 (when the Spanish had planted their first mission in California) to approximately 150,000 at the time of the American takeover. The reductions traced to the usual sources: diseases, combat, and colonial interference with traditional means of subsistence. But these losses paled next to those that occurred after 1848, when American settlers and officials openly proclaimed their intention to eliminate Indians in California. Mass killings by vigilantes, volunteer military companies, state militias, and federal troops, all with generous financial support from state and national governments, took a terrible toll. So did the destruction of villages and food stores, and the resulting exposure, starvation, and disease. By the 1860s, entire groups had been wiped out and fewer than thirty thousand Indians remained alive in the state.

In general, historians of colonial North America and the Great West have avoided labeling the destruction of Indians as genocide, holding that most of the deaths owed not to deliberate exterminations but to germs that were inadvertently spread. But the first decades of American rule in California present a case that meets the standards established by the 1948 United Nations Genocide Convention. During the Gold Rush, American authorities condoned and abetted the decimation of California Indians. Their words, their deeds, and their dollars allowed a genocide to proceed—and nearly to succeed.

Chapter 5
The whitening of the West

"What is the true significance of the word 'white'?" So inquired Pablo de la Guerra in 1849. De la Guerra was then serving as a delegate to the convention charged with writing a constitution for a new state of California. His query was prompted by a proposal to limit the right to vote in the new state to "every white male citizen of the United States, and every white male citizen of Mexico, who shall have elected to become a citizen of the United States." The specific inclusion of Mexican citizens was in keeping with a guarantee in the 1848 Treaty of Guadalupe Hidalgo, which had promised this right to those Mexicans whose place of residence had been transferred to the United States. Although the articles in the treaty and the proposed state constitution supposedly covered "Californios" like de la Guerra, the reference to color vexed him, veering as it did from Mexican precedent. "Many citizens of California," de la Guerra explained to his fellow delegates, "have received from nature a very dark skin; nevertheless, there are among them men who have heretofore been allowed to vote, and not only that, but to fill the highest political offices." How "unjust" it would be "to deprive them of the privilege of citizens because nature has not made them White." Of course, acknowledged de la Guerra, "if, by the word, 'white' it was intended to exclude the African race, then it was correct and satisfactory."

In the second half of the nineteenth century, de la Guerra's question echoed eastward from California. The shifting definitions of who was white and what that meant affected not only the privileges of citizenship but also where individuals lived and worked, what they were paid, with whom they associated, and even whether they could be in the region, now remapped as the western half of the United States, at all. The reconstruction of this West as American entailed the remaking of race relations, the establishment of the supremacy of the federal government, and the consolidation of an industrial capitalist order. With so much in flux and so much at stake, the whitening of the West incited intense debate, fierce resistance, and bloody combat.

The end of Indian independence

No group felt the forces of reconstruction and the power of the federal government more tellingly and terrifyingly than Indians. To make the West and its resources safe for white American settlers and for capitalist enterprise required that Indians, both those long resident in the region and those more recently removed to it, be dispossessed of most of their lands and then concentrated on reservations. From the Plains to the Pacific, armies of the United States battled Indians into submission, and federal agents took responsibility for restructuring native life. In government offices and among western settlers, the harshest foes of Indians called for and sometimes carried out California-style exterminations against native peoples. At the same time, self-proclaimed "Friends of the Indian" promised to save Indians from extinction by preparing them for a subordinated place in the newest West.

Although the reconstruction of western Indian life began before the Civil War, its full geographic impact was not felt until the latter half of the 1860s and 1870s. Along the Pacific slope, the arrival of American families in Oregon and gold-seekers in California resulted in the near destruction of numerous local Indian groups during the 1840s and even more during the 1850s. To the east, the pressure on Indian lives and lands was not yet so intense. So long as overland trail-goers were merely crossing the Plains, the Rockies, the Great Basin, and the Cascades or Sierras on their way to Oregon and California, incidents in which travelers and Indians attacked one another remained relatively rare. To be sure, the Oregon and California bound regularly denigrated Indians as savages and frequently accused them of theft. Indians, in turn, resented travelers who crossed their lands and consumed its resources without asking or paying for those privileges. Still, an uneasy peace generally prevailed. During the 1840s and 1850s, when hundreds of thousands of travelers made their way along overland trails, only a few hundred emigrants and a like number of Indians died in violent confrontations. But in the 1860s and 1870s, when Americans started to settle instead of pass through these lands and made clear their intention to monopolize its resources for themselves, wars ensued.

Compared with the Civil War, the casualties from the "Indian Wars" do not look very impressive. Between 1860 and 1890, the United States Army mustered about twenty-five thousand troops to fight Indians in twelve major campaigns. In approximately one thousand recorded engagements, the army reported a little under one thousand men killed. Estimates put Indian deaths at around three times that number. True, these figures leave out the tallies from operations waged by state militias and "irregular" units. As in Gold Rush California, these forces were often responsible for the most infamous massacres, like Sand Creek in Colorado, where no discriminations were made between "hostile" and "friendly" Indians or between men and women and children. Yet even with all the confrontations compiled, the carnage paled next to a major battle between Union and Confederacy. A single bloody hour at Gettysburg or Shiloh surpassed the casualties from decades of Indian Wars.

None of which diminishes the damages done to Indians or the desperation that drove them to battle an enemy who possessed great advantages in manpower and weaponry. Despite being outmanned and outgunned, Indians still won battles. Best remembered is the triumph of Sioux, Cheyenne, and Arapahoe fighters at the Little Big Horn in June 1876. But winning wars, in which numbers and technologies were so asymmetrical, was impossible, especially once the United States launched devastating assaults against Plains Indians' villages and food supplies. Slaughtering bison by the millions, Americans reduced them to near extinction and reduced Indians who depended on them to near starvation. The Comanches, long the most powerful nation on the southern Plains, surrendered by the mid-1870s. On the northern Plains, the victory at the Little Big Horn over Custer's Seventh Cavalry turned quickly into the last stand for the Sioux and their allies. Overall, the Indian population decreased from 350,000 in 1860 to 250,000 in 1890. Those who survived had little choice but to surrender their once vast holdings and the freedom these afforded for the confinement and impoverishment of life on reservations.

While most white Americans, particularly in the West, celebrated the vanquishing of native peoples, an influential minority lamented the losses and sought to prevent Indians from vanishing entirely. For some, the desire to avert complete destruction translated into efforts to preserve a record of "traditional" Indian life by painting and photographing it or by collecting artifacts and stories. Others envisioned a more thorough reformation as the Indians' only hope for salvation (in this world and the next). Following long-standing missionary practice, these reformers believed that Christianization and education were the keys to Indian survival. The Indian, explained the superintendent of one reservation, needed to be imbued with the "white man's ambition," to share "the objects and aims of a white man." Ideally, these lessons in whiteness would occur at boarding schools, where Indian children would be separated from the outmoded teachings of their parents. "If every Indian child could be in a [boarding] school for five years," contended one advocate, "savagery would cease and the governmental support of Indians would be a thing of the past."

4. A photograph of a Blackfoot man on horseback, taken by Edward Curtis in the 1920s. During his career Curtis photographed thousands of Indians, almost always garbing them in what he considered their traditional clothing. Like many artists and anthropologists of the era, Curtis presumed to capture native people and their ways before these inevitably vanished.

The desire to save Indians and to save on federal expenditures provided a dual rationale for breaking up reservation lands and allocating parcels to individual Indians. This was not a new idea; the Indians' would-be saviors had from the beginnings of the American republic insisted that only through the destruction of tribal communalism could the Indian be reconstructed as a private property–owning individualist fit for incorporation into American society. In the 1880s, with Indian landholdings fast decreasing and conditions on reservations perceived as rapidly deteriorating, the calls by "Friends of the Indian" for detribalization took on greater urgency. The Friends attained this goal with the passage of the Dawes General Allotment Act in 1887. Named for its author, Senator Henry Dawes of Massachusetts, chair of the Senate Indian Affairs Committee, the law redistributed reservation lands into individual parcels. Like the Homestead Act of 1862, the Dawes Act entitled the heads of Indian households to 160 acres. "At last," proclaimed Dawes, "there has been found a way to solve a problem which hitherto has been found to be insoluble" that "will wipe out the disgrace of our past treatment, and lift [the Indian] up into citizenship and manhood."

Few Indians shared Dawes's enthusiasm. Facing a bleak present and a dark future, many sought relief in alcohol. Others found hope in the visionary dreams of Wovoka, a Paiute who preached that if Indians lived harmoniously, shunned white ways (especially alcohol), and performed the cleansing Ghost Dance, the buffalo would return and Indians, including the dead, would be reborn to live in eternal happiness. Like Popé's vision of three centuries before and like those of numerous other Indian prophets in the intervening years, Wovoka's dream rekindled the hopes of desperate people. As word spread, increasing numbers joined in the ritual Ghost Dance, believing it would restore the good life that American colonialism had extinguished. Among the hopefuls was Sitting Bull, a revered Sioux chief, who was himself famous for his visions and his leadership in the victory at the Little Big Horn. Yet in December 1890, Sitting Bull died at the hands of Indian police at the Standing Rock Agency in South Dakota. A few days later, the Seventh Cavalry opened fire on Indians at Wounded Knee Creek on the Sioux's Pine Ridge Reservation (also in South Dakota). Sometimes characterized as the "last battle of the Indian Wars," the massacre at Wounded Knee killed 146 Indians, including 44 women and 18 children. With them went their dream of an old world restored.

Reconstructing races and rights

Struggles over the place of Indians were entwined with broader debates about race, rights, and the relationship between individuals, states, and the federal government that convulsed the United States in the last decades of the nineteenth century. In the case of Indians, their champions, while envisioning a path to citizenship, assumed that they would remain on the lower rungs of American society for the foreseeable future. Accordingly, boarding schools emphasized vocational training that would prepare Indian girls for domestic service and boys for menial labor. In many respects, the prospects for Indians in the American West paralleled the projects designed for uplifting emancipated African Americans in the postbellum American South. But sorting economic opportunities and setting racial orderings proved far simpler in the South than the West. In the former, race was largely a matter of black and white. With the advent of Jim Crow laws and the implementation of "one drop of blood" rules (which designated individuals with any African ancestry as black), stark demarcations came to rule most aspects of southern life. By contrast, the demography of the West defied easy bifurcations. As Pablo de la Guerra's query highlighted, the diverse origins of the West's population and the mixings among them produced a variety of complexions that complicated determination of who was white, who was not, and how to order such a motley assortment of peoples.

The presence of so many shades of skin among the population of the West owed to migrations and minglings both old and new. Long before any map showed the region as a "West" or as "American," relations between Spanish and French men and Indian women had made mestizos and métis more and more common. Add to that the long history of intercourse in Mexico with men and women of African descent, and it becomes clear how more than "nature" had made de la Guerra's fellow Californios so various in their complexions. American mountain men joined in the tradition of mixing. Many of the children of mountain men and Indian women moved back and forth between the cultures of their parents, taking advantage of the possibilities for brokering exchanges that came from having a place in two worlds. Although subsequent generations of American emigrants disdained such unions, the flow of people into the West, coming as it did from all directions in the second half of the nineteenth century, furthered the diversification of the population and compounded the challenge of racial ordering.

One way to simplify the complexities of a multiracial region was to lump those seen as not white or just deemed nonwhite together. This was the tactic taken by Hugh Murray, chief justice of the California Supreme Court, who ruled in the 1854 case *People v. Hall* that Chinese immigrants could not testify against white Americans. He based that decision on an 1850 provision that prohibited blacks and Indians from giving evidence against whites. Murray reasoned that "Indian" referred to anyone of the "Mongoloid" race and "black" to anyone who was not white. The ruling freed a white man who had been found guilty of murdering a Chinese man, since that conviction rested on now inadmissible testimony by a Chinese witness.

Linked to Native Americans by Murray's logic, the Chinese suffered discriminations and assaults second only to Indians. These began during the 1850s, when thousands of men from southern China fled the extreme poverty and political turmoil of their homeland to make the eastward journey to California, a supposed promised land that they referred to as "Gum Shan" (Gold Mountain). But once they reached the actual mountains and foothills of the Sierras, the Chinese encountered hostility and violence that chased them from the diggings or left them to work only the most marginal claims. During the 1860s, many Chinese gained employment on crews building the first railroad line across the West. Typically given the lowest pay and assigned the most dangerous tasks, Chinese laborers also endured considerable harassment. Anti-Chinese sentiment and action intensified during the 1870s and 1880s. Mobs attacked Chinese (most lethally in Los Angeles in 1871 and Rock Springs, Wyoming, in 1885) and drove them from towns across the West.

In California, where the Chinese population was most heavily concentrated, the rhetorical assaults against the Chinese grew more heated, particularly after the completion of the railroad line and the onset of a national economic downturn spread hardship and unemployment. Foreign in dress, language, and religion, the Chinese then became the most convenient scapegoat. Demagogues denounced them for their heathenism and servility, insisting that competition from slave-like "coolies" undercut the wages of free men. While demands for outright removal failed, the agitation that started in California and extended across the West galvanized sufficient support nationally to bring about the Chinese Exclusion Act of 1882. The law forbade Chinese laborers from entering the United States; it did not diminish the attacks, both verbal and physical, against the Chinese.

Before and after the Civil War, the specter of slavery haunted the West. Labor union leaders raised alarms about workingmen being reduced to "wage slavery." In the 1850s, opponents of Mormon control, first of Deseret and then of what was reconstituted as the Utah Territory, used the fear of white female slavery to assail the Latter-day Saints' practice of polygamy. In the rhetoric of the day, Mormon polygamy and African American slavery constituted the "twin relics of barbarism." During the late 1850s, the effort to assert federal supremacy led President James Buchanan to send troops toward Utah and brought the United States Army to the brink of battle against Mormon citizens. After the Civil War, with one of the twin relics vanquished, condemnations of the Mormons' peculiar institution of plural marriage took on even greater fervor. In the same year as the Chinese Exclusion Law, the Edmunds Act established fines and terms of imprisonment for men convicted of polygamy. Additional measures imprisoned some men, forced others to deny their plural marriages, sent hundreds of families into hiding, placed church assets in receivership, and put elections in Utah under the oversight of a federal commission. Finally, in 1890, the president of the Church bowed to national authority and directed Mormons to abandon polygamy.

Once their church leaders buckled, Mormons regained their political rights, and Utah soon advanced to statehood. In other cases, however, critiques of slavery were joined with denunciations of people who were clearly seen as not white. Such condemnations were evident in the anti-Chinese rhetoric of the 1870s and 1880s, as they had been in the efforts in the 1850s and 1860s to prevent the "African race" from establishing a foothold in the American West. Then lawmakers had enacted bans on slavery, while also prohibiting the entrance of free blacks into various territories and states. The exclusion of free blacks ran afoul of the federal constitution, but state legislators and local councils could and did curb the voting rights of African Americans, preclude their testimony in court against whites, and relegate them to segregated schools.

Yet the West remained a land of relative opportunity for African Americans, certainly compared to the South. Kansas held a particular allure for African-American migrants seeking new homes and farms outside the South, for that was where blood had been shed for the antislavery cause in the 1850s. And the Plains beckoned to African-American cowboys. Like Chinese immigrants constructing railroads, African Americans herding cattle generally earned the lowest pay among their fellow cowboys. Nonetheless, they enjoyed a degree of freedom on the open range that eluded blacks who stayed put in the South. The army offered African-American men another road to relative opportunity. Here, too, enlistees found themselves segregated into all-black units, save for the officers, who were white. But their valor in fighting Indians won them a modicum of respect from their commanders.

Largely unnoticed then was the irony of recently emancipated African Americans battling to end the freedom of Native Americans. Sadly, this was just one among many examples of destructive combat between nonwhite groups. Although sometimes lumped together by whites, nonwhites were often pitted against one another. The Irish, whose skin was fair but who were not generally regarded as wholly white, emerged as the most vocal and occasionally the most violent opponents of the Chinese. They were not alone, however. In the Los Angeles Riot of 1871, dozens of Mexicans participated in assaults against the Chinese. African Americans also joined in attacks, at least verbally, against Chinese "heathens." But mutual anti-Chinese sentiments, as well as shared darker complexions and mixed ancestries, built little solidarity among Mexicans and African Americans—as de la Guerra's endorsement of the exclusion of the "African race" from the privileges of citizenship attested.

The privileges to which de la Guerra maintained he and fellow Mexican Americans were entitled eroded considerably during the second half of the nineteenth century. As de la Guerra knew, article 8 of the Treaty of Guadalupe Hidalgo had guaranteed that "property of every kind now belonging to Mexicans" in territories transferred to the United States "shall be inviolably respected." But the treaty did not protect those properties or its owners from unjust taxation, uncertain titles, and exorbitant legal costs, which combined over ensuing decades to pressure many Mexicans to surrender their lands or sell them at discounted prices. Likewise, article 9 of the treaty pledged that former "citizens of the Mexican Republic" would enjoy "all the rights of citizens of the United States." But this provision, which appeared to deem Mexicans the equal of white Americans, did not account for the latter's biases against darker-skinned "foreigners." At the time of the Mexican-American War, proponents of manifest destiny had contended that the promiscuous mixing of European, African, and Indian blood had made Mexicans a "mongrel" race. By this logic, taking over Mexican land rescued it from an indolent people and put it in the hands of a pure and enterprising one. The censuring of mixed-race individuals became more pronounced after the war, which made it acceptable to use legal and extralegal means to dispossess Mexicans and deprive them of their guaranteed equality with white Americans. It also marginalized men and women, like the children of mountain men and Indian women, who had once straddled cultures and brokered exchanges.

In contrast with the various efforts to restrict the rights of those whose ethnicity, ancestry, or skin color rendered them insufficiently or uncertainly white, western territories and states took the lead in extending the franchise to women. Wyoming acted first in 1869, with proponents hoping that the right to vote would lure white women to a territory whose population tilted heavily toward males. A year later, the Utah Territory granted women the vote. Supporters of suffrage outside Utah expected that women would use their votes to overturn the practice of plural marriages. When the opposite proved to be the case, the U.S. Congress rescinded the right of Utah women to vote in 1887. But the West remained ahead of the rest of the nation in granting the franchise to women, though in a signal that white female suffragists shared the racism of white men, Susan B. Anthony questioned the wisdom of enfranchising Mexican-American women in Colorado. Still, Colorado granted women the vote in 1893, and Idaho followed in 1896. As in Wyoming, advocates claimed the ballot would attract white women to these states. And, more important, their votes would blunt the impact of the votes of African-American and immigrant men.

The Wild West

Scholars and the public alike have long been consumed by counting the bodies and accounting for the violence that beset the West in the second half of the nineteenth century. In the years after the Civil War, the West gained renown for being "wild," a reputation first established by dime novels and then spread by the purveyors of Wild West shows and later by the producers of filmed and televised Westerns. For generations, popular entertainment made it easy to explain violence by neatly distinguishing between good guys and bad and by seeing the "Wild West" as a clash between civilization and savagery, between law and disorder. Recent scholarship has accented broader social, economic, and political causes. The recognition of these forces diminishes the uplifting features once attached to western violence and ties it more accurately to the struggles over the primacy of the nation-state, the supremacy of the white race, and the ascendancy of industrial capitalism, struggles that embroiled the West and the United States in the last decades of the nineteenth century.

Consider vigilante movements, of which more than two hundred arose in the trans-Mississippi West between the onset of the Gold Rush and the beginning of the twentieth century. Participants claimed that vigilantism was an effort by concerned (and armed) citizens to bring order to lawless places. Since vigilantes, by their testimony, acted on behalf of their communities, they did not have to wait for a judge or jury to enforce justice: the hanged got what they deserved. This justification usually sufficed at the time and has continued to stand up in the court of popular history, where the swiftness of "frontier justice" has retained its appeal in many circles. But under scholarly scrutiny, the defense offered by vigilantes has unraveled. Studies of vigilante groups and their victims have revealed splits along ethnoracial, religious, class, and political lines. Indeed, by uncovering the white supremacist features of many movements, historians have revealed that western vigilantes were close cousins to the era's southern lynch mobs.

Or consider the most famous of western shootouts: "the gunfight at the OK Corral" in Tombstone, Arizona, on October 25, 1881. In an exchange of bullets that lasted only a few seconds (near but not actually at the OK Corral), the brothers Wyatt, Virgil, and Morgan Earp, along with John "Doc" Holliday, gunned down Billy Clanton and the brothers Tom and Frank McLaury. Billy's brother Ike survived but suffered another defeat when a judicial inquest exonerated the Earps and Holliday. Under the legal doctrine that increasingly prevailed in the American West, the Earps and Holliday had "no duty to retreat" in the face of threats posed to them by armed foes.

That verdict hardly closed the matter, leaving plenty of room for novelists, playwrights, filmmakers, and reenactors to dramatize the events in Tombstone and for historians to contextualize them. In its numerous fictionalized restagings (especially for the screen), the shootout has gotten extensively lengthened, and Wyatt Earp (who ended his career in Hollywood) and his team have usually been venerated as honorable lawmen (though in more revisionist treatments acknowledged as bartenders and brothel-keepers). The many films about the OK Corral, as well as hundreds of other Westerns that feature comparable duels, have made gunfights seem an everyday occurrence in the Wild West. Not so, according to historical research. Towns like Tombstone, where the discovery of precious metals precipitated a rush of men, witnessed lots of brawling, which often turned lethal, thanks to ready access to firearms. But the extraordinarily high homicide rates in boomtowns like Tombstone were not matched in the other setting most favored by Westerns—"cowtowns" such as Dodge City, Kansas. There the meeting of cattle trails and rail lines brought a seasonal influx of cowboys. As in mining towns, the presence of so many single men and the abundance of alcohol triggered ample fighting. Yet the carnage was far more contained because local constabularies generally disarmed cowboys before allowing them into the town's saloons.

While sudden quarrels born of spirits-fueled disagreements incited some of the violence in the West's wildest places, deeper and more enduring rifts were also at work. At the OK Corral, the Earps were not so much the agents of law as they were the representatives of a particular order, a cabal made up of the town's merchants and mining magnates. Their foes were cowboys, whose agrarian ways this new order threatened. By the disorder they created, the Clantons and the McLaurys resisted—until the Earps' guns made Tombstone safe for an industrial capitalist regime.

The gunfight at the OK Corral was one of hundreds of bloody episodes that involved struggles over the incorporation of the West into the American nation and over the command of the region's resources. Best remembered are the range wars, because these, too, have been the subject of hundreds of Western films. They pitted homesteading, fence-building farmers against open range livestock herders, or large ranchers against small ones, or cattlemen against sheep raisers.

Often the economic dimensions of the competition for foraging lands overlapped with ethnic and religious divisions. Thus, in parts of the Great Basin, Basque sheepherders contended with white American cattlemen. On the New Mexico range, the attempts by white American cattle raisers to take exclusive control put them in conflict with Mexican-American livestock raisers and farmers, whose claims, often based on communal traditions, typically predated the Mexican-American War. To defend their rights, bands of Mexican Americans dressed in white capes and masks cut the barbed-wire fences that white American ranchers and railroad companies erected to mark off their lands. Between 1888 and 1892, the activities of the Gorras Blancas (White Caps) made them outlaws, at least in the eyes of American authorities, but not in the eyes of their fellow Nuevomexicanos, who cheered their banditry and sheltered them from arrest.

In these and numerous other cases involving conflicts over western resources, the claims of white Americans rested on problematic legal grounds. Mexican Americans pointed to the precedence of their usage and to the promises of the Treaty of Guadalupe Hidalgo, while Basques asserted their equal rights to lands that were in the public domain. But white American cattlemen had advantages their rivals could not match. They had the money to hire gunmen to enforce their claims, and they had the American nation-state as their ally.

In the last decades of the nineteenth century and the early years of the twentieth, western laborers of all complexions and creeds learned a similarly hard lesson about the weapons of the wealthy (including courts and contracts) and the allegiances of the nation-state. Over this period, large corporations assumed an ever larger role in the economic development of the West, especially in the extraction, processing, and transportation of the region's natural resources. These corporations' expansion ran against a long history of suspicion of corporations and posed a challenge to the American dream of achieving independence. In politics and protests, labor leaders invoked those American traditions and railed against wage slavery. At the same time, corporate leaders drew on another American tradition by employing workers of different ethnicities and playing them off against one another. Ethnic tensions undercut the solidarity among industrial workers and hampered the growth of labor unions.

Faced with wage cuts and lethal working conditions (industrial accidents claimed a much higher body count than the gunfights so celebrated in western lore), workers did come together to stage a number of strikes, the largest of which targeted mining and railroad corporations. To protect their property and combat unions, employers hired private armed forces. When these alone could not do the job, corporate magnates called for reinforcements, and state militias and federal troops entered the fray. In the era's bloody battles between capital and labor, the latter almost always suffered greater casualties, while the former benefited from the power and privileges that Pablo de la Guerra had recognized to be the "true significance" of being white in the American West.

Chapter 6
The watering of the West

His name was Francis G. Newlands, and the surname fit.
A congressman from Nevada, Newlands was the chief sponsor of
the 1902 Reclamation Act. The legislation, often referred to as
the Newlands Act, established a National Bureau of Reclamation
and charged this agency with constructing dams and irrigation
projects in the western United States. By these works, the
Newlands Act, trumpeted its proponents, would reclaim the
region from arid nature, opening new lands for farmers and
restoring the American dream for generations to come. It did not
turn out that way, but millions of hopes and dollars continued to
be invested in the conquest of the Great American Desert.

The watering of the West involved more than hydraulic
engineering. It rested as well on faith. That was attested to by the
biblical metaphors its advocates employed. Reclamation, it was
said, would transform an inhospitable desert into a fertile garden,
would create a "promised land," would deliver "salvation." The
watering of the West required belief in new "scientific"
propositions, many of which turned out to be dubious. It entailed,
too, assigning added responsibilities to experts, often in the
employ of the federal government, who took charge over not only
the manipulation of western waters but also the management of
western lands and the regulation of other natural resources.

All this made westerners ever more dependent on federal stewardship and federal expenditures—and ever more resentful of federal oversight.

A broken promised land

The Newlands Act was hardly the first time that government action summoned extravagant rhetoric and unrealized expectations about the transformation of the West and the salvation of the nation. A century earlier, Thomas Jefferson had prophesied that the vast West would safeguard the agrarian virtue of the United States by offering "room enough for our descendants to the thousandth and thousandth generation." In the succeeding generation, similar pronouncements about the future of the West as a haven for family farmers attended the enactment of federal laws that lowered the price of land, reduced the minimum acreage required for purchase, stretched installment payments over more years, and granted some squatters the right to "preempt" ownership of property that they had farmed. The chorus of cresting hopes peaked with the passage of the 1862 Homestead Act, which offered 160 acres of "free" land to those who would occupy and improve it.

Yet time and again, the actual workings of these laws did not deliver on these promises. In the early republic, wealthy, well-connected speculators obtained the most land and the best land. Later in the nineteenth century, railroad corporations took the blame for thwarting the dreams of yeomen. The lobbying (and bribes) of these enterprises secured them over 175 million acres from federal and state governments. For railroad executives, this was fair inducement for extending tracks across the continent; for their enemies, it was evidence of the corruption of American government. There was much truth in these allegations. Still, in the last decades of the nineteenth century, environmental hurdles played as large a role as political treachery in undermining the promises made on behalf of western lands.

The obstacle was the Great American Desert, the designation by which Americans disparaged the territories that the United States had acquired first through the Louisiana Purchase and then by the Treaty of Guadalupe Hidalgo. Prior to the Homestead Act and the construction of railroad lines to the Pacific, most of this region lay beyond the realm of American agriculturalists. In the middle of the nineteenth century, the United States was home to around one and a half million farmers, fewer than 8 percent of whom lived west of the Mississippi River. (These numbers did not include Indians, many of whom were, of course, farmers.) The vast majority of these farmers worked soils just to the west of the Mississippi or in the eastern parts of Texas. In the 1840s and 1850s, would-be farmers edged further out onto the Plains, despite misgivings about the fertility of prairie and the expense of fencing land where wood was scarce. Still, farmers largely remained to the east of the 100th meridian, where the Great American Desert was thought to become too arid for agriculture. Far more farmers headed to the Pacific slope, where wetter climes beckoned. Only in the Mormon settlements in the Great Basin did American farmers establish an agricultural colony in the heart of the Great American Desert.

Not agriculture but other opportunities initially lured settlers into (as opposed to across) the Great American Desert. As in California, precious metals were a particularly powerful draw, and the Gold Rush set a pattern for subsequent mining bonanzas. New strikes in Colorado, Nevada, Montana, and the Dakotas also inspired large numbers of men (and a handful of women) to hurry to these sites in pursuit of quick fortunes to be made from mining or from selling goods and services to miners in the towns that sprang up around diggings. As in California, riches eluded most prospectors. The earliest phase of rushes in which individuals could excavate metals with minimal equipment and expertise soon yielded to more heavily industrialized means of extracting ore, and boomtowns generally busted when mines gave out.

While mines came and went, the mining industry flourished in the interior West. At the end of the century, this industry accounted for 10–15 percent of employment in Colorado, Idaho, Montana, and Arizona. Gold and silver held the most glamour, but copper and coal mines became ever more important as the industrialization of the nation progressed.

Likewise, while many mining camps disappeared, more enduring mining centers birthed metropolises that continued to attract industry, commerce, and people. San Francisco and Denver were the largest of the cities that outlived their boomtown origins, but they were not alone in acting as magnets for migrants. So great was the growth of cities and towns in the West that by the end of the nineteenth century the region boasted a higher proportion of urban dwellers than any other part of the United States save the Northeast.

The growth of cities and the development of mining (as well as other industries generally based on the extraction and processing of various raw materials) offered no comfort to those who clung to older variants of the American dream. This was not the West as Thomas Jefferson had imagined its future to the thousandth generation. His "empire for liberty" depended on this region being populated by yeoman farmers, who were in Jefferson's creed the "chosen people." A region dominated by urban dwellers and industrial wage workers seemed instead the realization of Jefferson's worst nightmares.

Preferable from the perspective of latter-day Jeffersonians were the inroads made by livestock raisers. While farmers remained wary of the Great Plains, stock raisers more readily embraced it as a fenceless feeding ground for cattle and horses. Following the Civil War, cowboys moved hundreds of thousands of head of cattle north from Texas to take advantage of the abundant forage and to deliver fattened stock to rail depots in Kansas. With Indians being confined to reservations and bison slaughtered to near extinction, cattlemen took control over more and more of the Plains and sent more and more animals to graze on the open range.

What followed was a familiar pattern in the nineteenth-century West: an enterprise that rose with the extraction of an abundant resource declined or was forced to move on to new locations when nature's bounty gave out. That had happened to the fur trade when overtrapping reduced the supply of beavers, and it repeated in the booms and busts that followed the discovery and depletion of minerals at one or another site. For cattle, the introduction of so many head overwhelmed the grasses on which the animals depended.

For the post–Civil War cattle industry, the problem of overgrazing was compounded by other environmental challenges. In drier years, grasses withered during the heat of summer droughts, while harsher winters on the Great Plains took an even greater toll on animals. The worst came in 1887, when a prolonged deep freeze killed millions of stock. This "great die up" left the western cattle industry reeling.

Competition from farmers and their fences contributed as well to the closing of the short-lived heyday of the open range. Further enticements from the federal government helped farmers overcome their fear of grasslands. Responding to complaints about the inadequacy of 160-acre parcels in semiarid terrain, Congress passed modifications to the Homestead Act that offered larger tracts. New technologies also persuaded farmers to cultivate the Plains, as machines made planting and harvesting more efficient and the invention of barbed wire reduced the cost of fencing fields.

Along with these new laws and new equipment, railroad corporations encouraged farmers to take up lands in drier parts of the West. After receiving immense land grants to build multiple lines across the western half of the United States, railroad companies faced the challenge of selling their acreage and creating customers for their freight-hauling services. Aggressive and deceptive marking campaigns followed that hyped scientific studies and technological advances. Real estate agents for railroad companies touted "dry farming" as one answer to the problem of too little rainfall. They also proclaimed that the improvements brought by Americans would answer farmers' prayers for more precipitation. Rain, railroad propagandists contended, "would follow the plow." That is, turning over the soil would release moisture into the air. So would the steam generated by railroad engines. The result would be more rainfall and positive, permanent climate change.

For a while, faith appeared to be rewarded. In the 1870s and early 1880s, the Great Plains enjoyed wetter than normal years, tempting more farmers to take up lands in areas previously considered too arid. But in the late 1880s, drier conditions returned. A drought in 1889 ruined many farmers, who discovered to their dismay that dry farming worked best in wet years. Or as one popular lament put it, "in God we trusted, in Kansas we busted."

Reclamation and conservation

Even as boosters waxed optimistic about the transformation of the Great American Desert, others offered more downbeat assessments about the malleability of the West's nature. These observers insisted that rather than simply altering the West, Americans must alter their ways. They recognized that supplies of water and other vital resources were limited and needed to be managed differently. This led in the last decades of the nineteenth century and the first decades of the twentieth to challenges to customary legal doctrines governing the appropriation of water. More far-reaching were shifts in attitudes and political economy as conservation of a permanent public domain and irrigation of the West became national priorities.

Particularly prescient were the observations of George Perkins Marsh and John Wesley Powell. Marsh's 1864 volume *Man and Nature* linked the rise and fall of civilizations around the ancient Mediterranean to the use and depletion of forests and other natural resources. The book contained a clear moral for his contemporaries: if the United States failed to curb the destruction of woodlands and take more care of watersheds, it faced a collapse similar to those of Greece and Rome (and, though he did not know it, Cahokia). Powell's message came in the form of an 1878 government report based on his surveying expeditions along the Colorado River. As Powell explained, aridity precluded the importing of traditional American practices into the West. Instead of the unfettered enterprise and small family farms that Americans venerated, successful settlement of these lands required greater regulation and more collective undertakings, especially in the construction and upkeep of irrigation works.

Powell found a hopeful example in the agricultural outposts established by Mormons around the Great Basin. The Mormons, Powell noticed, had built irrigation systems that provided sufficient water for thousands of farms. They had done so with little capital, equipment, or engineering expertise, overcoming these deficiencies through cooperative efforts under the auspices of their church. For Powell, the Mormons' ability to bring hundreds of thousands of acres of desert land under cultivation reinforced the importance of collective enterprise and centralized supervision for water projects.

The Mormon model and other examples of irrigation from around the world did not, however, gain much favor among Powell's compatriots. Because most Americans fixated on the theocratic dangers and heretical doctrines of the Church of Jesus Christ of Latter-day Saints, especially the practice of plural marriages, they were not disposed to accept the wisdom of the Mormons' water works. So, too, a global survey of irrigation projects in comparably arid regions yielded disturbing findings. Yes, world history provided evidence of how technology and engineering allowed agriculture to expand into previously inhospitable areas. And yes, in recent times, the British had made India a showcase for the possibilities of dams and irrigation. But these cases, both historical and contemporary, suggested that the more elaborate and grandiose the effort, the more despotic was the regime that carried it out and the more concentrated was the wealth and power that resulted from it.

While this was certainly not the society that most Americans sought, the desire for irrigation projects that could open more western lands was very strong. In the last decades of the nineteenth century, some farmers did emulate Mormon practices, banding together to construct small-scale systems. More often, westerners looked to county and state governments to undertake water projects. Still, by the end of the nineteenth century, most conceded that the scope of work overwhelmed the capacities of these entities. "Great storage works," explained President Theodore Roosevelt, "are necessary" but "too vast for private effort" or individual states and so "properly a national function." Roosevelt's endorsement built support for Newlands's bill, which had the added attraction of paying for itself through proceeds from the sale of public lands made more valuable by irrigation. At the same time, the Reclamation Act comforted those who feared the centralization of power and the further monopolization of resources by stipulating that no single owner could purchase water to irrigate more than 160 acres.

The Newlands Act, which inaugurated a new era in the damming of western rivers, is best understood as part of a broader shift in attitudes and policies about the western economy and environment. From the beginnings of European colonization of the Americas, newcomers treated nature as something to be exploited. The failure of Indians to fully profit from the resources around them was a frequently invoked justification for their dispossession. This mindset, which viewed wilderness as waste and nature as needing improvement, prevailed through the first century of the United States. It found expression in policies that opened the public domain for private gain and in judicial decisions that privileged the development of natural resources over the preservation of them. So long as Americans believed that new frontiers awaited their exploitation, they had little reason to question these attitudes or amend their actions. After the Civil War, however, alternative ideas earned a wider hearing. The judgments of Marsh and Powell, which reckoned with the limits of natural resources, increasingly resonated among American elites, if not yet among ordinary western Americans.

As the nineteenth century drew to a close, the sense that an era had ended and a new, uncertain one begun pervaded American arts and letters. That partially explained the appeal of the grand landscape paintings of Albert Bierstadt and Thomas Moran, which exalted and exaggerated the majesty of western mountains and canyons, while erasing any signs of the "improvements" that were transforming western scenery. The paintings and sculptures of cavalry, cowboys, and Indians by Frederic Remington and Charles Russell carried as well a nostalgic tinge. More directly capturing the zeitgeist, historian Frederick Jackson Turner used the Census Bureau's 1890 announcement that the frontier had closed as a starting point for an 1893 essay that identified the frontier as the explanation for all previous American development. In this brief paper on "the significance of the frontier in American history," Turner celebrated the ways in which the settlement of successive Wests had nurtured American democracy and molded the enterprising and pragmatic character of the American people. The announcement that the frontier had passed gave his essay an elegiac quality, leaving in doubt what would happen to these characteristics in a postfrontier future. Turner's fellow historian of the western experience, Theodore Roosevelt, shared these concerns. An easterner whose own experience as a rancher in the Dakota Territory made him an exponent of the "strenuous life," Roosevelt worried that absent the tests that came with "winning"

5. This gold-plated Colt revolver belonged to Theodore Roosevelt. On one side of the handle is the monogram "TR"; on the other is a buffalo head, in celebration of Roosevelt's experiences as a rancher in the Dakotas and a hunter. Roosevelt's time on the Plains shaped his enthusiasm for the rugged tests of manhood that "the winning of the West" imposed. He championed these views in the histories of westward expansion that he wrote and in the conservation and reclamation policies he put in place when he served as president of the United States.

Wests, American men, confined to urban settings, would slide into effeminacy.

In politics, Roosevelt championed imperialism abroad and conservation at home as the antidote to emasculation and the foundation for a more sustainable extractive economy. He gloried in the manhood-making aspects of military combat and spoke anything but softly in favor of acquiring colonies overseas that could keep United States expansionism alive, while also providing new markets for American products. With the last acquisition of territory by the United States dating to the purchase of Alaska in 1867 (from Russia for the price of two cents per acre), and with Americans now filling arable lands from sea to sea, Roosevelt looked beyond the continent for the next phase of American expansion. His attention fastened on the Caribbean and the Pacific. Both of these areas had long drawn the attention of American expansionists, but at the end of the nineteenth century the focus gained renewed force. Roosevelt applauded the annexation of Hawaii in 1898 and, during the Spanish-American War, put words into action, leading his contingent of "rough riders" into battle in Cuba. As president, Roosevelt remained steadfast in his support for the projection of American power beyond the North American mainland.

Domestically, he pushed hard for protecting "wilderness" areas in conditions like those portrayed by Bierstadt and Moran. A sojourn in unspoiled places, he believed, would give Americans the opportunity to replay the national epic of heroic struggle with nature that had made the United States great—at least while on vacation from their more mundane, urban jobs. The practice of safeguarding the most monumental landscapes had commenced decades earlier with the setting aside of Yosemite Valley in 1864 and the creation of Yellowstone National Park in 1872. Another milestone arrived with the passage of the 1891 Forest Reserve Act, which placed some lands in the West under permanent federal ownership and supervision. Roosevelt's administration considerably expanded both these initiatives, adding 110 million acres to the forest reserves, which after 1905 came under the aegis of the newly christened United States Forest Service.

Headed by Gifford Pinchot, the Forest Service served as a model for a new age in which federal officials oversaw a permanently public domain. The supervision by federal agents was not meant to end extraction of resources from these lands. Rather, the "gospel of efficiency" that Pinchot instilled in his agents sought to regulate logging and grazing and protect watersheds through scientific management. Thus did Pinchot's Forest Service promise to revitalize the nation. Its expert balancing of conservation and regulation would ensure the long-term health of America's natural splendors and the long-term wealth of the industries that depended on finite resources in a postfrontier era.

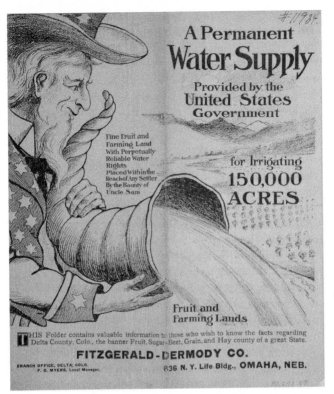

6. This brochure nicely captures the promise that federally supported irrigation would turn regions previously considered too arid for agriculture into "fine fruit and farming land" with "a permanent water supply provided by the United States government."

Watering in the early twentieth century

For all the anxieties about an era ending, the closing of the frontier and the turning of the century brought more evolution than revolution in policies and practices. Conservation and reclamation certainly enlarged the federal footprint in the West.

In practice, though, conservation proved more conservative and reclamation less radical than proponents had hoped or opponents feared. Although denunciations of federal interference with the free enterprise of westerners grew louder, government agencies generally accommodated extractive interests. And in spite of the Newland Act's provisions directing reclamation's benefits to small farmers, agribusinesses and urbanites were the clearest winners in early twentieth-century water wars.

One sign that the times were not really changing was the continuing influx of homesteaders. In the first two decades of the twentieth century, homesteaders laid claim to more acreage than during the entire nineteenth century. In part, this was because homesteaders could now claim more acreage, thanks to a 1909 law that doubled the amount of land available to individuals. The federal government further encouraged homesteading by reducing from five years to three the time that claimants had to wait to gain title to their properties. By the 1920s, these inducements helped propel a new surge of farmers who pushed agriculture into the higher and drier portions of the Plains and the even more arid Southwest.

Even where federal policies precluded additional transfers of public lands, the workings of government agencies perpetuated many long-standing practices. Forest Service agents faced considerable hostility from timber executives and ranchers. The anti–federal government rhetoric directed at them was often heated. But Forest Service management was not really so threatening. The ethos of efficiency, after all, valued sustainable development. Regulation also curtailed the cutthroat competition that destabilized extractive enterprises. Moreover, prominent resource users found their way onto local forest advisory boards, positions from which they could strongly influence decisions about logging and grazing capacities.

The Newlands Act similarly did not live up to its revolutionary billing. Although the Bureau of Reclamation completed a number of impressive projects that expanded western agriculture, the restrictions on who received the water from them were readily evaded. In the early twentieth century, the concentration of landholdings proceeded. Agribusinesses rather than yeoman farmers dominated the region more than ever.

Nowhere were these trends more apparent than in California. That state's agricultural production grew to lead the nation, but small family farms were few. The agricultural workforce was instead peopled by seasonal migrant laborers, often immigrants from Asia and Mexico. Their impoverished, transient existence little resembled the yeoman ideal elevated by Jefferson and supposedly resurrected by Newlands. Yet through the first third of the twentieth century, the conditions of agricultural laborers in California attracted relatively little public notice or political attention.

What did cause an uproar in California and beyond was the 1906 application by municipal authorities in San Francisco to construct a dam across the Tuolomne River in Hetch Hetchy Valley. After the devastation of that year's earthquake and fire, San Francisco officials saw the project as essential to the rebuilding. Although the dam would flood a portion of Yosemite National Park, its benefits in the form of abundant and affordable water and electric power for the Bay Area's growing population clearly outweighed the loss of a remote section of Sierran wilderness. That, at least, was how San Francisco's leaders viewed it, in accord with the utilitarian calculus employed by conservationists like Gifford Pinchot. Unexpectedly, however, the plan ran into fervent opposition led by naturalist John Muir. Like Pinchot, Muir was close to Theodore Roosevelt. In fact, Muir and Roosevelt toured Yosemite together in 1903. But Muir insisted that the preservation of unspoiled wilderness served a higher purpose than efficiency and long-term economic sustainability. For Muir and those who rallied behind his banner, the damming of Hetch Hetchy was akin to destroying "the people's cathedrals and churches, for no holier temple has ever been consecrated by the heart of man."

The battle over Hetch Hetchy raged for years. Congress approved the project in 1913, but opponents did not relent in their campaign to halt construction. When the dam and aqueduct were completed in 1923, they delivered water and power more than 150 miles away to San Francisco and surrounding communities. Still, the intense debates revealed enduring divisions within the ranks of conservationists. Disappointed about Hetch Hetchy, Muir's followers readied for future fights to preserve, as opposed to simply conserve, the nation's scenic "temples."

While San Francisco's designs on Hetch Hetchy grabbed headlines, municipal leaders in Los Angeles more quietly schemed to bring water from afar to their city. Founded by Spanish missionaries and soldiers in 1781, Los Angeles had remained a small village with a predominantly ranching economy through the Spanish and Mexican eras. There was little indication that this status would change during the first decades of American rule. Without a natural harbor or a navigable river into the hinterland, Los Angeles lacked the attributes on which other nineteenth-century American cities rose. Only the most deluded civic promoters predicted that it would ever rival San Francisco or even San Diego as a Pacific metropolis. But the arrival of railroad lines and the expansion of citrus growing brought a population and economic boom in the last quarter of the nineteenth century. Turning delusion into reality, boosters built a harbor that furthered Los Angeles's remarkable spurt. With its population passing one hundred thousand in 1900, the growth outran the supply of local water available from the often dry Los Angeles River. As in San Francisco, real estate interests and city officials looked to the Sierras. Their focus fastened on the Owens River along the eastern slope of the mountains, and there Los Angeles agents secretly commenced buying up leases.

By the time ranchers and farmers in the Owens Valley discovered the plot, it was too late. Their protests, including attempts to destroy the aqueduct from the Owens River to Los Angeles, failed to stop the project. Unlike Hetch Hetchy, the fate of the Owens Valley also failed to galvanize a national movement. In 1913, waters from the Owens, traveling across 233 miles of harsh desert and over several mountain ranges, first reached Los Angeles. Agriculturalists in the Owens Valley were left high and dry. Los Angeles, by contrast, maintained its extraordinary ascent, surpassing San Francisco to become the West Coast's leading city. The population of Los Angeles vaulted over the 1 million mark in the 1920s.

The rivalry between San Francisco and Los Angeles overshadowed the commonality between them in the struggles for water. In both cases, as in the workings of the Newlands Act, the watering of the West favored those with wealth and power. In the West, as the saying went, water flowed uphill to money.

Chapter 7
The worldly West

The 1965 Immigration Reform Act, predicted the *Wall Street Journal*, ensured "that the new immigration pattern would not stray radically from the old one." Few forecasts proved so wrong so quickly. In the decades after the law came into effect, the pattern of immigration into the United States and particularly into the western states that bordered the Pacific or Mexico changed dramatically. These post-1965 flows significantly altered the national origins of the region's population. Along with the twentieth-century transformations wrought by global wars and globalized commerce, the new immigration amplified the connections between the West and the world.

What emerged as "the West" in the latter half of the nineteenth century had numerous claimants prior to its incorporation into the United States; by the twentieth century, those rivals had retreated, and at least some westerners fought hard to protect the West from foreign influences. Like the growing import of the national government in the affairs of the West, the international presence generated resentments and efforts at restriction, most directly in the realm of immigration. Yet, in the second and third quarters of the twentieth century, the region's fate was increasingly defined by federal interventions and entwined with international developments.

Washington, the world, and the West
between the wars

In the first decades of the twentieth century, federally directed conservation and reclamation projects did not stop the unstable swings and unsustainable practices that had long shaped (or misshaped) the development of the West. The backlash that gathered against the intrusiveness and failings of the federal government and other "foreign" interests only partially concealed the reality of how dependent westerners were on the largesse that flowed from the nation's capital and on the capital that came from Wall Street and other outside investors. Washington and Wall Street offered ready targets for the wrath of westerners. Immigrants presented an even more convenient, and more vulnerable, scapegoat.

The rhetorical salvos against Washington and Wall Street and the exclusionary impulses toward "non-Americans" were not new. In the last decades of the eighteenth century, American settlers in the First West railed against the national government for its inability to chase out Indians and clear away Spanish and British interference and for the favoritism it showed to absentee speculators at the expense of actual settlers. A century later, as a protracted economic downturn gripped the region, the portrayal of the West as a "plundered province" held in colonial subjugation by federal authorities and their capitalist confederates rallied millions of westerners to the Populist banner. Hard times also heightened the intensity of attacks against nonwhites and catalyzed the anti-Chinese movement that claimed the Exclusion Act of 1882 as the first victory in the battle to close the West to Asians.

The return of better times diminished but did not end the resentments. The onset of World War I raised demand for a variety of western goods. Farmers on the Great Plains planted more wheat to feed armies and civilians in Europe. Loggers in the Pacific Northwest harvested more trees. Across the region, farms, factories, and mines stepped up production, and residents, both urban and rural, enjoyed unprecedented prosperity. Labor shortages elevated wages and encouraged employers to look south of the U.S. border for new workers. Already in the decades before the war, the pull of wages that were many times those paid in Mexico lured an increasing flow of immigrants from Mexico into the American Southwest. Higher wartime wages, together with the violence that accompanied the Mexican Revolution, made the move across the border even more attractive.

Still, labor unrest and ethnic animosities continued to flare and combined most ferociously in Bisbee, a copper mining town in the southeastern corner of Arizona. There, in late June 1917, the International Workers of the World (IWW) launched a strike against the Phelps Dodge Corporation. Corporate officials and local authorities claimed that the "Wobblies," as members of the IWW were called, were radicals (which they were) and that the strike was "pro-German" (which it was not, though the strikers included a large proportion of immigrants). Early on the morning of July 12, a posse of more than two thousand men arrested approximately the same number of strikers. Those who refused to renounce the IWW and return to work were herded at gunpoint into manure-laden railroad cars. Nearly thirteen hundred men, mostly foreign-born and including many of Mexican ancestry, were forcibly expelled from Bisbee and stranded almost two hundred miles away in Hermana, New Mexico.

After World War I ended in November 1918, the economy again slumped, and crackdowns against labor unions, radicals, and immigrants swelled. During the "Red Scare" that erupted in 1919, government agents particularly targeted Wobblies, most violently at Centralia, Washington. A clash on the first anniversary of the Armistice left five dead. Across the nation, immigrant radicals were rounded up and deported thousands of miles to their countries of origin. Although the economy soon recovered, the prosperity of the 1920s bypassed much of the rural West, with the prices of many western commodities remaining depressed. For immigrants, the 1920s brought no return to normalcy. Insisting that many of the foreign-born who had come into the United States over the last half century were either un-American or not capable of being Americanized, "nativists" campaigned for reductions in the number of immigrants allowed into the country and restrictions on the places whence they came. The nativists' crusade won passage of the 1924 National Origins Act. This law reached back to the 1890 census to set annual quotas on immigration based on the national origins of the American population thirty years earlier. That severely curtailed future entrants from the southern and eastern European countries— Italians, Jews, Slavs—who had dominated more recent immigration. The law also almost entirely barred further immigration from Asia. In the same year, the United States finally granted citizenship to American Indians and also formalized the Border Patrol, whose primary charge grew to stopping Mexican as well as Chinese people moving north from Mexico.

For Mexican immigrants and Mexican Americans, the force of the new immigration regime hit home when the stock market collapsed in 1929 and the Great Depression ensued. Unlike the 1920s, when hard times were largely confined to the countryside, the Great Depression of the 1930s distressed urban as well as rural Americans. Westerners took particularly hard blows. Of the ten states registering the greatest decline in income during the Depression, seven were in the West. In California, where booming oil production and the rise of Hollywood had made the twenties a roaring time, the Great Depression quickly reduced large numbers to poverty and put one in five residents on government relief by 1934. Hispanic families, many of whom eked out precarious livings as transient agricultural laborers during good times, found the going even tougher during the 1930s. But rather than extend relief to some of the hardest hit, the administration of President Herbert Hoover opted for deportations. Because government agents had trouble determining the status of many Mexicans, the roundups conducted by the Immigration Service netted both those who had entered the United States illegally and American citizens of Mexican ancestry. The latter faced the burden of proving their right to remain in the United States. Altogether, the federal government deported over eighty thousand people. An additional five hundred thousand Mexicans, fearful of being caught in raids and unable to obtain employment or relief, retreated south of the border.

The plight of agricultural laborers—their flight from devastated homelands, their hopes for a better life in the American West, the discriminations, disappointments, and often desperate poverty they instead encountered as migrant workers—gained greater public attention during the 1930s. In many ways, these had been the experiences of generations of immigrants from Mexico, China, Japan, and the Philippines. What was new in the 1930s and what became the subject of songs by Woody Guthrie, photographs by Dorothea Lange, and the novel *The Grapes of Wrath* by John Steinbeck was that these workers were white Americans. Lumped together as "Okies," though Oklahoma was one of several adjacent states from which they hailed, the heroes and heroines of Guthrie, Lange, and Steinbeck were plain folk from the Plains. They had fled the ecological catastrophe of the Dust Bowl and the economic calamity of the Depression in search, like so many before them, of a fresh start in California. But they met hostility from locals and found only sporadic work and meager wages from growers.

Like other westerners, these victims of the Depression were assisted by a splurge of federal spending during the New Deal. While western states were disproportionately represented on the list of declining incomes, they also topped the charts when it came to calculating per capita benefits from federal expenditures between 1933 and 1939. Indeed, the top fourteen states on this list were in the West. The construction of roads, bridges, and government buildings created jobs for the unemployed and raised incomes throughout the region. Even more important for the West and its infrastructure were the reclamation and conservation projects the federal government undertook, with enormous hydroelectric dams on the Colorado and Columbia Rivers serving as potent symbols of what a good deal the New Deal was for westerners.

Most westerners acknowledged this largesse with their votes, which swung the region solidly behind Franklin Delano Roosevelt in the elections of 1932 and 1936. This did not mean westerners ceased to carp about the contradictions in federal policies that expended vast sums on water projects to increase harvests while simultaneously paying farmers to take lands out of production so as to raise crop prices. More bothersome were new rules and regulations that interfered with westerners' freedom to conduct their private enterprises as they had on public lands. The Taylor Grazing Act of 1934, which ended homesteading and brought stock-raising on federal lands under government management, was a particular sore point for ranchers. Infringing on the customary practices of livestock raisers, the Taylor Act underscored the growing presence of the federal government, as well as the dependence of even the most individualistic of westerners on it.

The West as arsenal

The impact of the federal and the foreign on the West surged during World War II and the Cold War. Although restrictions on immigration, patrols of borders, and deportations of Mexicans were supposed to cordon off the West from the world, the barriers remained permeable. Following the bombing of Pearl Harbor, the removal of Japanese Americans from their homes along the West Coast signaled the latest in a long line of efforts to shut those deemed un-American out of the West. Yet the West continued to grow more connected to the world, its economy increasingly dependent on the region's role in defending the nation against its foreign enemies. That meant the West was also more reliant on Washington. The federal dollars that funded the development of the military infrastructure and the research and production of weapons were key to the West's prosperity during the middle decades of the twentieth century.

The American military and American Wests had matured together. In the republic's first decades, American troops explored western territories, checked European rivals, battled Indians, ushered removals, safeguarded pioneer settlements, and conquered Mexico. Through the nineteenth century, except during the Civil War, the United States Army was by and large a western army. Its posts secured American claims across the continent, and its payments to soldiers and suppliers pumped money into frontier economies.

During World War II and the Cold War, what set apart the military's presence from that of earlier times was scale; the number of people directly engaged in these war efforts and the amount of dollars dwarfed nineteenth-century figures. In addition, unlike in the nineteenth century, the mid-twentieth-century West was home not only to military bases but also to the plants that manufactured many of the most advanced weapons of war. During the four years when the United States was directly involved in World War II, Washington provided 90 percent of the investment capital that allowed private corporations in the West to expand exponentially their production of ships, planes, and other weapons. The infusion of federal funds did much the same during the decades of Cold War, enabling the continuing growth of defense-related industries and the development of new ones.

In the global conflicts of this era, first against fascism and then against communism, the United States faced foes with designs for territorial and economic aggrandizement that bore at least some resemblance to the history of American westward expansion. Indeed, some in Nazi Germany and Imperial Japan saw the

United States as a model for how to conquer hinterlands, cleanse them of ethnically "savage" inhabitants, and colonize them with settlers. In the Soviet Union the United States found an ally during World War II and an enemy in the Cold War whose history of territorial spread, dating back to the Russian Empire, eclipsed its own.

Another troubling parallel, at least on the semantic level, emerged with the issuing of Executive Order 9066 by President Franklin Roosevelt in February 1942. The order authorized the relocation of West Coast Japanese to what were termed concentration camps. A response to the hysteria that gripped the United States in the wake of Pearl Harbor, it led to the uprooting of more than one hundred thousand Japanese immigrants and Japanese Americans from their homes in California, Oregon, and Washington. The internment camps, as they were renamed to erase the link with Nazi concentration camps, did not starve, work, or gas inhabitants to death. The order did, however, compel people whose only crime was their national ancestry to leave their homes in haste, often with no time to secure the value of their property. Sent to generally inhospitable and inaccessible parts of the interior West, the internees spent much of the war living in barracks behind barbed wire fences.

The homes and neighborhoods the interned left behind quickly filled and overfilled with a flood of newcomers attracted by the opportunities that the war had opened on the West Coast. Pacific ports served as the principal staging ground for soldiers, sailors, and pilots heading out to fight Japan. Many of those harbors also became shipbuilding centers. The number of jobs in San Francisco Bay Area shipyards leapt from 4,000 just before the war to 260,000 at the height of production. Still greater were the openings in Los Angeles–area aircraft manufacturing plants. The demand for labor in these operations was so immense that the private corporations that ran them initiated extensive and expensive efforts to recruit and retain workers. That entailed

7. The noted documentarian Dorothea Lange took this photograph in Oakland, California, in March 1942. The store's owner, a Japanese American, had put the sign up on December 8, 1941, the day after Pearl Harbor, but the store closed when its owner was sent to an internment camp.

raising wages and introducing new benefits such as medical insurance and paid child care. It also meant employing workers previously shut out from these industries. Women entered the paid workforce in large numbers, occupying approximately 25 percent of the jobs in shipyards and 40 percent in aircraft plants. Encouraged by corporate recruiters, Native Americans left reservations and African Americans fled the South to work in war industries in West Coast cities. In Seattle, where there were opportunities in both shipbuilding and aircraft industries, the black population increased from four thousand before the war to forty thousand at its conclusion.

Although West Coast cities did not import all of the legal and extralegal mechanisms that buttressed the Jim Crow regime in the

South, the convention of restrictive covenants in housing deeds (that prohibited owners from selling or renting homes to people of particular races or religions) and the power of customary prejudices severely constrained the places where nonwhite newcomers could live. A fraction moved into the residences that Japanese had left behind, but most struggled to find adequate and affordable housing, given the limited choices of neighborhoods. Those neighborhoods that did allow nonwhites soon experienced the strains that came when too many people lived in too little space.

The squeeze was greatest in California, whose population jumped 75 percent between 1940 and 1943. Neighboring states witnessed population booms of their own, as wartime industries were decentralized across the Pacific Coast, Southwest and Mountain West states. Only the Plains states lagged in enjoying the fruits of federal investment and the enduring frictions that came with populations galloping upward.

Even with extraordinary recruitment campaigns and a new rush of people moving west, demand for labor still outran supply in various sectors of the western economy. In agriculture in particular, employers turned again to Mexico. A 1942 deal between the governments of the United States and Mexico set the terms for laborers to cross the border on a temporary basis. Although the agreement promised guest workers prevailing wages, most received much lower pay than that. They also had no way to challenge the system, for braceros (manual laborers) had no right to negotiate their own wages and faced deportation if they left the jobs for which they had been contracted.

The bracero program outlived its wartime origins, as did a number of the economic and demographic changes World War II instigated. Unlike the past, when the cessation of hostilities had halted the economic stimulus that warfare generated, the end of World War II brought only a brief cooling. With the Cold War commencing soon after Japan's surrender, the national government's defense budget quickly returned to a war footing. Once again, the West received far more than its share of armament contracts and armed forces installations. The manufacture of military aircraft and the emergence of aerospace and missile technologies spurred the expansion of those industries and of the places in which they were located. First and foremost, that continued the astonishing growth of Los Angeles, but it also stimulated the economies and augmented the populations of San Diego, Seattle, Phoenix, Denver, Dallas, Fort Worth, Houston, and Wichita. Although the shipbuilding industry that underwrote the San Francisco Bay Area's boom during World War II did not regain its previous heights of production, the technologies needed for advanced airplanes and missiles spawned the electronics and computer industries that grew up around Stanford University. In addition to the Silicon Valley, the partnership between research universities, private enterprises, and federal funds for military projects fostered the emergence of other "high-tech" centers across the West. That combination, along with the availability of vast amounts of public land, made the West the center for nuclear weapons. That began with the basing of the Manhattan Project at Los Alamos, New Mexico, during World War II. It continued with the mining of uranium in the Southwest, the manufacturing of plutonium at Hanford, Washington, the testing of atomic weapons in Nevada, and the basing of intercontinental ballistic missiles underneath the Plains.

All of this contributed to the post–World War II westward tilt in the American census. At the end of the war, around 10 percent of Americans lived in the West. That proportion nearly doubled during the decades of the Cold War. California saw the largest increases, and in 1962 it surpassed New York to become the nation's most populous state. Texas also experienced a postwar rush, which allowed its population to overtake New York's in 1994.

In California, Texas, and across the West (and the nation), people on the move headed to suburbs, drawn to these burgeoning communities by their own dreams and by inducements from the national government. Boosted by federal policies that subsidized mortgages and guaranteed loans, private homeownership came within reach for millions. Suburbanization gained additional encouragement with the passage of the Interstate Highway Act of 1956. More than connecting states together, the new roads, 90 percent of whose costs the federal government paid, provided the means by which suburban dwellers could commute to downtown workplaces. As subdivisions supplanted farms, ranch houses, rather than ranches, became the symbol of the good life in the postwar American West.

The world returns to the West

After 1965, California and the West continued to gain people and grow in proportion to the rest of the nation, but the sources of those additions shifted. As in earlier decades, most of the newcomers during World War II and over the next twenty years had come west to become westerners. Following the 1965 Immigration Reform Act, however, the westward current was overtaken by northward and eastward flows. In these same years, the economy of the West was also reoriented, with Asia becoming ever more important to the region's (and the nation's) enterprise.

Abolishing the discriminatory quotas that had severely constricted immigration from all but northwestern Europe since the 1920s, the 1965 Act allocated 170,000 places to people from the Eastern Hemisphere and 120,000 to those from the Western Hemisphere. More important, the legislation exempted persons with close relatives who were citizens of the United States from these restrictions. Thus, immigrants who had become American citizens were now able to reunite their families.

This system of giving preference to family members resulted in a surge of immigration from Asia and Latin America. The quota for immigrants from Mexico was set at twenty thousand per year, but more than four times that number annually gained entry because of the family preference rule. Tens of thousands of Central Americans also took advantage of this provision. Meanwhile, tens of thousands of other Latin Americans moved across the southern border of the United States without legal permission, swelling the Latino population of the West and the nation. Asians' numbers rose even more dramatically. Whereas they had accounted for only about 6 percent of immigrants in the decade before 1965, they represented nearly 30 percent in the following years. Within these ranks, places of origin shifted as well. Chinese and Japanese had dominated the Asian-American population since the nineteenth century, but after 1965 Koreans, Filipinos, and South and Southeast Asians became more prominent.

By the mid-1980s, this new immigration had transformed the demographic profile of the West. The Latino population in the nineteen most western states jumped to 15 million. In the same period, immigration tripled the Asian-American population, which reached 5 million by 1985.

The demographic changes were most dramatically registered in California, nowhere more than in Los Angeles. At the end of the nineteenth century, approximately three-quarters of the population of Los Angeles had been born in the United States. Unlike other fast-growing American cities that received millions of immigrants during the last decades of the nineteenth century and first decades of the twentieth, the percentage of foreign-born in Los Angeles remained stable, even as the population of the city increased twelvefold between 1900 and 1930. Despite a sizeable movement of Mexicans into Los Angeles during and after the Mexican Revolution, the census of 1930 recorded the Latino population as only 8 percent of the city's inhabitants. Asians composed only about 2 percent.

Contrast this with the situation after 1965, when approximately one in four legal immigrants to the United States settled in

California. The rush led *Time* to dub the Los Angeles airport the "new Ellis Island." By the late 1980s, the foreign-born population of Los Angeles had surpassed that of New York City.

Economic shifts accompanied these demographic ones. Most apparent was the growing importance of the Pacific Rim to western business. In one regard, this was not new. After all, the West began as a search for a better route to the East. Still, the last decades of the twentieth century saw a rapid rise in the value of trade between the United States and countries on the other side of the Pacific. For American consumers, it seemed as if the long-sought passage to Asia had been attained as they reaped the benefits of cheaper goods made across the Pacific and imported to the United States.

These changes came at a cost, and they generated a backlash. Across the West, anti-immigrant sentiments flared up. English-only movements gathered momentum, renewing old ideas about how to "Americanize" immigrants. More punitive were campaigns against illegal immigrants. These movements sought to stem the flow of unauthorized immigrants by enhancing the enforcement abilities of the Border Patrol. They also targeted those already here by pushing for deportations and passing legislation to deny public benefits to undocumented immigrants. Still, the demand for cheap labor overwhelmed efforts to stem the continuing movement of people across the Mexican-U.S. border.

The same was true of the flow of goods across the Pacific. During the last decades of the twentieth century, a pronounced imbalance between imports and exports emerged, with the former eclipsing the latter. This surge of manufactured goods from Asia contributed to the deindustrialization of the American economy in the 1970s and 1980s. As factory jobs disappeared and unemployment rates rose, calls for restrictions on imports joined calls for restrictions on immigration. But the lure of cheaper products proved more politically powerful than the protectionist sentiments that underlay the fight to limit foreign items.

By no means were these trends unique to the West. Immigration and globalization reshaped the whole of the United States. The West, though, because of its proximity to the Pacific and to Mexico, felt these pressures more acutely. Try as some did to wall the West off from the world, these protections against foreign people and goods, like the projections of borders on earlier maps, did not hold.

Chapter 8
The view from Hollywood

The first chapter of this book began in the middle of North America at the Gateway Arch, its panoramic views offering a vantage point from which to contemplate multiple Wests and to conjure homelands before they became Wests; this final chapter takes its figurative roost on Mt. Lee in Los Angeles. What gives Mt. Lee its renown are the uppercase letters on its southern slope. First erected in 1923, the sign initially spelled out "HOLLYWOODLAND." Shortened in 1949, its forty-five-foot tall letters spread across 350 feet now proclaim that "HOLLYWOOD" lies below.

As the global capital of mass entertainment, "Hollywood" has become a symbolic homeland for hopes and dreams. Yet like so much of the western past in which projections and realities have become entangled and distorted, the glitter of "Hollywood" the dream factory can obscure the grit of Hollywood the place. From atop Mt. Lee, it's hard to get the close-up that would reveal the challenges of getting ahead and getting along in the most diverse of western American cities. Still, at least on smog-free days, the view from Mt. Lee extends across much of the Los Angeles basin and to the Pacific Ocean, a perch that encourages some observations about the recent history of the American West and concluding thoughts about the deeper history introduced in these pages.

The view on screen

Like "the West," "Hollywood" connotes more than a current location. As a stand-in for the entertainment industry that supplied images of the West to the world, its roots can be found in nineteenth-century paintings, photographs, dime novels, and Wild West Shows. What changed about the imaginings in the twentieth century was the reach of cultural productions. Beginning with the 1903 movie *The Great Train Robbery*, "Westerns" dominated American cinema for a good part of the twentieth century. Although *The Great Train Robbery* was shot in New Jersey, moviemaking soon shifted to Los Angeles; the ample sunshine of southern California was conducive to outdoor shooting and its open, arid landscapes were appropriate for Westerns. During the 1960s, when the genre lost favor with Hollywood studios, foreigners put their own stamp on it. The most American of genres, Westerns, as the Italian director Sergio Leone recognized, now "belong[ed] to the world." And far more than any scholarly statement, Westerns, whether made in Hollywood or abroad, influenced popular understandings of the western past.

In style and substance, many of the classic Westerns of the twentieth century took a pose and a page from their nineteenth-century antecedents. Motion pictures lifted shots and camera angles from still pictures; characters and plots followed dime novel formulas. These put white men front and center. Nonwhites and women of all races were relegated to secondary roles, or no roles at all. Heroes were strong and silent, rugged individualists who were quick on the draw and ready to shed blood to secure civilization's triumph over savagery. No one embodied this ideal better than John Wayne.

Wayne and Westerns peaked in influence and popularity in the years after World War II. Between 1945 and 1965, Hollywood studios released around seventy-five Westerns each year—about one-quarter of the films they made. Television featured Westerns

8. A souvenir postcard from around 1909 shows a lineup of cowgirls from the 101 Ranch in Oklahoma. The 101 was a working ranch that covered more than one hundred thousand acres, but it was best known for the Wild West shows it began to stage in 1905. Like Buffalo Bill's troupe, the 101 Ranch Company featured cowboys, cowgirls, and Indians (including Geronimo) and played to audiences across the United States and Europe.

even more prominently. On the small screen at the end of the 1950s, twenty-eight series set in the "Old West" were on the weekly prime-time schedules of the major broadcast networks. These accounted for seven of the ten most highly rated programs. With the advent of the Marlboro Man in 1954, advertisements reinforced the message of Westerns. Like the characters played by Wayne (and the image he projected offscreen), the Marlboro Man was a self-reliant, sharpshooting cowboy who exemplified the ideal of American manhood.

In the latter part of the 1960s, changing times and tastes diminished the appeal of Westerns. Hollywood studios cut back significantly on the number of Westerns they produced; networks looked to other genres to fill out prime-time schedules. The Westerns that were made increasingly upended traditional formulas. In these "anti-Westerns," the clear distinctions that had once separated white-hatted heroes from black-hatted villains gave way to grayer portrayals. Indians received more sympathetic treatments. Violence, formerly venerated as essential to the winning of the West, lost its redemptive justifications.

While the enthusiasm of Americans ebbed, Europeans remained enamored of Westerns. Ever since William Cody (Buffalo Bill) had toured the Continent with his Wild West Show, Europeans had embraced things western. In Germany, Indians particularly fascinated. The German novelist Karl May's books set in the Old West continued to sell long after his death in 1912 and after the Western went into decline in the United States. Europeans also made their own movies about the West's wildness. Most notable were the so-called spaghetti Westerns of Sergio Leone. These shared in the revisionist spirit of the era's anti-Westerns, but Leone's productions had a visual style that was unique. Filmed in Spain, based on Japanese movies, and starring a cast of American, Italian, and Yugoslav actors, Leone's movies attested to the internationalization of the Western.

Back in the United States, the sprawl of suburbia supplanted the wide-open spaces of the Old West on big and small screens. In focusing on life in the subdivisions that sprouted around Los Angeles (and, to a lesser degree, every other American city), Hollywood productions returned to the original purpose of Hollywood. The original "HOLLYWOODLAND" on the famous sign, after all, had advertised not the capital of the motion picture industry but a suburban real estate development. In fact, "the industry," which in Los Angeles came to mean the entertainment industry, had long promoted real estate interests by bolstering the local economy and by disseminating images of the good life in twentieth-century southern California.

Depictions of an older West diminished but did not entirely disappear. To some extent, Westerns relocated, with science fiction films and television series transferring classic plots, characters, and settings to the "new frontier" of space. Nonetheless, in the last quarter of the twentieth century, cowboys were much less visible than they had once been, especially after bans on cigarette advertisements removed the Marlboro Man from television.

Even as Wayne's star waned and Westerns faded on American screens, westerners, some playing up their cowboy credentials, raised their profile on the national political scene. Of the twenty-two men nominated by the Democratic and Republican parties for the presidency in the elections from 1952 and 2012, eleven hailed from or were primarily affiliated with one of the nineteen western states (whose ranks, after a forty-seven-year break following the admission of New Mexico and Arizona, expanded in 1959 to include Alaska and Hawaii). That westerners made up half of the major party candidates reflected the tilt of the American population to those western states. That Ronald Reagan and George W. Bush, in the tradition of Theodore Roosevelt, often dressed and talked as if they came straight from the range to the stump suggested that the mythic cowboy hero still resonated with American voters, even if a shrinking percentage lived in the still wide-open spaces of the rural West or had seen many Westerns.

The close-up

At street level, the harsher realities of urban life press into view in Hollywood. True, Hollywood's grime, crime, poverty, prostitution, homelessness, and hopelessness are hardly unique. They exist in many parts of Los Angeles and most of the inhabited places of the modern American West.

What is distinctive, at least in degree, is the heterogeneity of the populace in Hollywood and surrounding districts of Los Angeles. Ethnic enclaves such as Thai Town and Little Armenia are both parts of Hollywood. To the east of Hollywood are Los Angeles's Filipinotown, Chinatown, and Little Tokyo. South from

Hollywood is a vast and expanding stretch known as Koreatown and the small district of Little Ethiopia. To the west is Little Persia, whose growing population has led some to tag the Westside of Los Angeles as Tehrangeles. Across the Los Angeles basin, dozens more neighborhoods show up on maps with one or another ethnic/immigrant label. But like so many boundaries in the western past, the mappings that neatly delineate various "Littles" and "Towns" mask the fluidity of borders. The prevalence of polyglot mixes is not a new phenomenon, though post-1965 immigrations have certainly augmented the diversity of neighborhoods and the complexity of cultural blends.

Earlier in the twentieth century, Boyle Heights, on the Eastside of Los Angeles, epitomized the perils and possibilities of urban diversity. Attracting an assortment of newcomers in the first four decades of the twentieth century, this working-class neighborhood assembled Mexicans, Japanese, African Americans, European immigrants, and, most numerous of all, Jews. Most came to Boyle Heights because its housing was more affordable and did not carry the restrictive covenants that kept those deemed "nonwhite" (a category that still included most Jews in the early decades of the twentieth century) out of more well-heeled neighborhoods in Los Angeles. In the eyes of authorities, this ethnic variety was alarming. A 1939 report by a federal housing agency condemned the neighborhood for its "diverse and subversive racial elements" and determined that Boyle Heights was "hopelessly heterogeneous."

To government officials, heterogeneity made Boyle Heights a bad risk for housing loans, but within the community, bonds developed across ethnic and religious lines. At the local high school, clubs formed to foster intergroup mixing, and youths especially enjoyed challenging their elders' conventions by trespassing cultural boundaries. From these tentative youthful crossings, more enduring alliances emerged, some personal, through intermarriages, and some political, through the creation of organizations that made common cause for civil rights.

World War II and its aftermath tested these connections. Executive Order 9066 removed the Japanese, leaving homes and apartments hastily vacated and reducing the enrollment of the area high school by a third. Into this void came wartime migrants, including significant numbers of African Americans and Native Americans, attracted by jobs in defense industries. When the Japanese won release from the internment camps, they often found their return to former homes blocked by more recent arrivals. After the war, the diversity and unity of Boyle Heights suffered from the suburban sprawl that reshaped Los Angeles and other metropolitan areas. Gaining access to the privileges of whiteness, Jewish residents of Boyle Heights relocated to newly developed tracts in the greener (and whiter) Westside and San Fernando Valley of Los Angeles. Immigrants from Mexico (and later other countries in Central America) filled the places left by Jews. Meanwhile, metropolitan planners fixed on Boyle Heights as a place through which to build highways. By 1960, five freeways cut through the neighborhood. These facilitated traffic between downtown Los Angeles and points east and south and encouraged developers to supplant citrus groves with suburban homes. The construction of highways, though, physically divided Boyle Heights, with "white flight" and new immigration turning the neighborhood more Latino year by year.

An outbreak of arson and violence in the summer of 1965 in the Watts section of Los Angeles reinforced the national tendency to see metropolitan patterns and problems in black and white. The episode began when the arrest of an African-American motorist set off an outcry against decades of mistreatment at the hands of the almost all white Los Angeles police force. Several days and nights of violence followed, leaving thirty-four dead, more than one thousand injured, and $40 million of property torched across an eleven-square-mile area. Along with other conflagrations that erupted in cities across the United States during the second half of the 1960s, the Watts riot called attention to widening racial fractures between white and black, rich and poor, and suburbs and cities.

The lines between white and nonwhite in Los Angeles and the West were, of course, more complicated, which became more apparent in the years after 1965 and came into fuller view when another "race riot" broke out in the spring of 1992. As in 1965, the events of 1992 had their immediate origins in a traffic incident. In the latter case, a high-speed chase ended with white police officers beating Rodney King, an African-American man, as he lay prone on the pavement. Although the brutality was captured on video, the perpetrators were acquitted, a verdict that caused simmering rage to boil over. Beginning in South Central Los Angeles, looting and arson spread over the next six days to other parts of the city. By the time a semblance of peace was restored, fifty-five people were dead, fourteen thousand arrested, and eighteen hundred treated for gunshot wounds. Property damage surpassed $1 billion.

During the 1992 riot and in its immediate aftermath, many in the media cast the disorder as a reprise of 1965, but closer scrutiny revealed important differences that attested to the changing demography of Los Angeles. Although both eruptions started in South Central Los Angeles, what had been a mostly black neighborhood in 1965 was no longer so in 1992. Its population was now approximately 50 percent Latino, and police records showed that this group accounted for 43 percent of those arrested, compared with the 34 percent who were African American. The targets of arsonists had also shifted. In 1965, around 80 percent of looted and burned stores had belonged to white (mostly Jewish) shopkeepers. By 1992, Jewish merchants had largely fled the area, while Korean-run businesses proliferated in South Central Los Angeles. Attacks on these stores reflected the animosities that had developed between African Americans and Korean Americans, particularly in the wake of the 1991 shooting of Latasha Harlins, an African-American teenager, by Soon Ja Du, a Korean-American shopkeeper. Yet much of the damage to Korean businesses occurred not in South Central but in Koreatown itself, where the residential population and those charged with arson and looting were mostly Latinos.

Even more than the Watts Riot of 1965, the violence of 1992 stained the reputation of Los Angeles, a metropolis whose remarkable ascent rested on the sunnier face it generally presented to the rest of the world. That Los Angeles became a great city—the foremost crossroads in western North America for peoples and products from north, south, east, and west—confounded expectations, providing a model that inspired emulation and condemnation. Unlike Cahokia, which was situated near the confluences of the continent's major rivers, or the other metropolises that subsequently could claim to be the continent's greatest gathering points, Los Angeles had none of the attributes that major cities typically possessed. Driven instead by the dreams of its boosters, by waters from afar, by federal investments in national defense, and, after 1965, by a new flood of immigrants, Los Angeles overcame its geographic disadvantages.

Defying the cycles of boom and bust that had characterized so much previous western development, the city and surrounding area registered staggering gains in census after census. Its sprawling, automobile-centric development found imitators across the West and the nation. At the end of the twentieth century, Los Angeles was also the most ethnically diverse metropolis in the United States, boasting the largest communities of Mexicans, Salvadorans, Guatemalans, Koreans, and Filipinos outside their homelands. It had truly become the place where the world congregated. This was fitting because for decades Los Angeles, through "Hollywood," had exported the western American fantasy to the rest of the world. But in the ashes of the spring of 1992, this dream took on a nightmarish tone for the peoples of Los Angeles.

The long view

On May 1, 1992, a tearful Rodney King stepped in front of a battery of cameras and microphones and issued a plea heard round the West and the world: "Can we all get along? Can we,

9. John Gast's 1872 painting *American Progress* was commissioned to illustrate a western guidebook and was widely reproduced, making it one of the most familiar depictions of westward expansion.

can we get along?" With Los Angeles then ablaze, the answer to King's query seemed an emphatic no. Indeed, with people who had come to the American West from the American South, from south of the United States, and from across the Pacific belittling and battling one another, the events of 1992 apparently validated the conclusion of the 1939 housing agency: heterogeneity was hopeless.

This dystopic perspective from late twentieth-century Los Angeles contrasts with long-standing visions of the American West as a land of promise and progress. The legends that previous generations printed (and screened) about the American West conveyed hope, not hopelessness. Thus, in the early 1870s, Brewster Higley wrote the poem "My Western Home," and for generations people have sung of a mythic range in which "seldom is heard a discouraging word." Around the same time that Higley penned his homage to the cloudless skies of the Kansas grasslands, John Gast painted *American Progress*. At the far left of Gast's canvas, Indians and bison slide into the shadows. In their place march a parade of pioneer types and the vehicles that carried them westward across the plains: prospectors and farmers, a covered wagon, a stagecoach, and a railroad train. Above floats an angelic female figure, carrying a schoolbook and stringing a telegraph wire to uplift and connect the nation from coast to coast. A few decades after Higley and Gast, Frederick Jackson Turner turned poem and picture into several thousand words that told a similar tale about western promise and national progress.

Notably absent from Higley's poem, Gast's painting, and Turner's prose is evidence of the bloodshed that accompanied the westward expansion of the United States. All three expunged or considerably downplayed that aspect of American advance across the continent. In Higley's poem, "the Red man was pressed from this part of the West." In Gast's picture, Indians retreat quietly from the scene. Likewise, Turner paid little attention to the wars that won the West. In his scheme, the frontier brought Indians and pioneers into close, if temporary, contact. But the pioneers' encounters with Indians and their adaptations to "primitive" conditions were only a transitional stage that laid the groundwork for taming wilderness and transforming it into productive farms and bustling towns.

By no means did all historical presentations turn a blind eye to violence. Turner's contemporary Theodore Roosevelt embraced it: allowing that the shedding of blood was not always "agreeable," he insisted that it was the "healthy sign of the virile strength" of the American people. As historian and president, Roosevelt exalted in "our manifest destiny to swallow up the land of all adjoining nations who were too weak to withstand us." He deemed it "desirable for the good of humanity at large that the American people should ultimately crowd out the Mexicans from their sparsely populated Northern provinces" and take the rest of the West from Indians too.

Historians of American Wests have now disavowed such claims on behalf of manifest destiny. Like the anti-Westerns that challenged older cinematic staples, the last half century of scholarship has inverted triumphant takes on the history of American Wests. Recent scholarship has tended to lament what historian Patricia Limerick has labeled the "legacy of conquest" and to spotlight the victims of American expansion.

In its simplest iteration, this legacy as a chapter in the longer history of European colonialism in the Americas can be distilled into two maps: the first showing the entirety of the Americas as Indian countries, the second shading only the tiny fraction of the United States currently reserved for indigenous communities. While the government of the United States maintained the fiction that American Wests were won through contracts, not conquests, the treaties with Indian nations (and, for that matter, with the Mexican nation) paid a pittance for acreage that was usually expropriated at the equivalent of gunpoint. Accompanying and closely correlating to the loss of land was the loss of people. True, the catastrophic fall in Indian numbers in the centuries after 1492 owed more to disease than to warfare, but a collective autopsy still finds that colonialism was a chief cause of death.

As with so many stories we tell about American Wests, this one requires elaboration. In the streamlined version that features only death and dispossession, a long story is made short. It banishes to a static and irrelevant "prehistory" all that came before the coming of Europeans. This version further misleads by treating the claims of European empires and the American nation as facts on the ground and not the fantasies they remained for varying durations. The long story prematurely turned short erases Indian countries from maps, missing entirely the ways in which for generations the territories of some Indian peoples expanded before they contracted. This story downplays the strategies Indians employed to contest colonial incursions and contain foreign impositions. Finally, it dismisses the adaptations and accommodations with

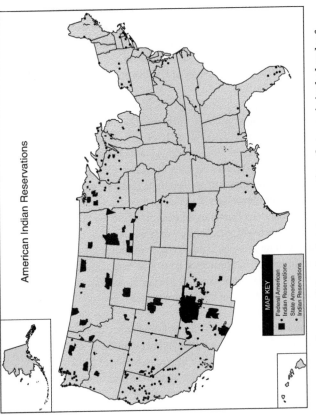

American Indian Reservations

MAP KEY
· Federal American
  Indian Reservations
■ State American
  Indian Reservations

10. This map shows the federal and state reservations that remain in the hands of Indian communities today. Almost all of the 324 federally recognized reservations are in the western half of the United States.

which Indians defied the doom that their friends and foes predicted for them a century ago.

Contrary to once prevalent views, Indians have not vanished. Instead, the census count for American Indians, which had fallen to 250,000 in 1890, slowly rebounded during the first half of the twentieth century, reaching 350,000 in 1950. Over the next fifty years, the census of American Indians registered more significant gains, topping two million in 2000. In 2010, more than five million Americans told census takers that they were at least partly American Indian.

In addition to their numbers, the hopes of Indians have been raised by the advent of casinos on reservations. In 1987, two small Native American nations in the desert outside Los Angeles won a Supreme Court case, turning back the claims of California and the federal government to prevent their gaming centers from becoming full-blown casinos. Their success sparked a national trend in American Indian development, where the fantasies of another western city, Las Vegas, were replicated on the slivers of land held by American Indians in many parts of the country. Profits from casinos stimulated economic revival and funded efforts at cultural renaissance, at least on those reservations that were close to major population centers.

But these gambling venues also triggered fights about tribal enrollment. Bitter divisions emerged between those who met blood requirements and those who were excluded from membership and denied a share of gaming profits. In Oklahoma, the controversies have been particularly acidic. There, the descendants of the African-American slaves of removed Indians have met continuing resistance in their efforts to gain enrollment in the tribes they consider their kin.

With attention focused on glitzy casinos and the newer opportunities and conflicts they generate, the grimmer realities of Indian life on most reservations often escape notice. Yet, at the beginning of the twenty-first century, statistics present a familiarly depressing portrait. Poverty rates among Indians far exceed the national average. So does unemployment, which reaches 80 percent on some reservations (where federal support provides the only jobs and the only buffer against starvation). Poor nutrition, disease, alcoholism, and suicide all contribute to lowered life expectancies, which fall well below the nation's norms.

During the twentieth century and continuing in the twenty-first, Indians increasingly moved away from reservations. Although federal policies swung back and forth between encouraging the breakup of communal landholdings and tribal governance and trying to protect the autonomy and integrity of reservations, the push of poverty and the pull of outside opportunities steadily drew Indians away from tribal reserves. By century's end, three-fifths of American Indians lived in cities. Not surprisingly, given its magnetic power, Los Angeles boasted the largest Indian population of any American city.

In Los Angeles and the other metropolitan areas to which they moved, Indians tended to blend. Rather than "Little Native Americas," American Indians usually resided in multiethnic neighborhoods, sharing spaces and struggles with millions of others, some migrants like themselves, others immigrants from abroad. In these urban settings, particular tribal identities often gave way to a more general pan-Indian identification. But the blurring of distinctions went further than this, for urban Indians, like their neighbors, frequently consorted across ethnic lines.

As the long view exposes, ethnic crossings and cultural blendings were not new to American Indians or to the history of American Wests. Trade networks and traditions of intermarriage, captivity, and adoption opened precolonial Indian societies to items, ideas, and individuals from outside their ranks. With the arrival of Europeans and Africans, these tools for incorporating foreign goods, beliefs, and people expanded. Of course, Europeans exerted their own incorporating agenda. But while missionaries tallied their baptisms, the results of their efforts looked more like cultural convergences than outright conversions.

That preference for convergence over conversion prevailed through the colonial era and persisted into the period of the westward expansion of the United States. To be sure, pressures against the mixing of peoples built under the American regime, which sought to define races more precisely and to confine those deemed nonwhite into separate social and legal categories. These efforts did lead many American Indian groups to alter their traditions of membership, which had typically incorporated adopted captives on the basis of their cultural adaptation. Beginning in the late nineteenth century and taking on renewed meaning a century later, some Indians embraced the American system by using blood percentage as the essential criteria for enrollment. Nonetheless, the governments of the United States and its western states never fully succeeded in their sorting projects or in simplifying the demographic and cultural complexities that arose when people of differing origins and heritages shared the same space.

Nor have efforts to wall off the American West from the rest of the world ever created an enduring seal. The permeability is especially evident on the border between the United States and Mexico. While the Gasden Purchase in 1853 completed the territorial adjustments between the two nations, the permanence and security of the border has remained an issue. At times, the idea of restoring the pre-1848 border has inspired hopes and fears. One such moment came in 1915, when word of a "Plan of San Diego" circulated in south Texas and northern Mexico. The plot called for an insurrection by a "liberating army of peoples and races." Press reports distorted the reality of this army, but combined with rumors that Germany was trying to induce Mexico to declare war against the United States, the newspaper stories reinforced concerns about the sanctity of the border and the loyalties of Mexican immigrants and Mexican Americans in the Texas borderlands. More recently, an advertisement for a brand of vodka that mapped Mexico's boundaries as they were before 1848 and as they might be again "In an Absolut World" triggered an Internet sensation. This uproar was largely confined to virtual space, but in the real world the battle to protect the border has been waged with bigger budgets for the Border Patrol and with the construction of a new fence across the boundary between the United States and Mexico.

To its proponents, the fence is the only way to keep the West American, but in many respects the projection runs contrary to much of the history of American Wests. Across the centuries, migrations and minglings of peoples have triggered struggles that have torn families and societies apart. Yet, dark and bloody as western grounds have often been, the longer view also offers examples of convergences in which common ground was found— at least for a while. Those episodes of concord, from colonial frontiers to multiethnic neighborhoods in the modern American West, provide evidence of barriers breached and accords reached, of people overcoming their differences instead of being overcome by them, of heterogeneity made hopeful.

References

Chapter 2: Empires and enclaves

Indian informant speaking to a French missionary about beavers:
Reuben Gold Thwaites, ed., *The Jesuit Relations and Allied Documents: Travels and Explorations of the Jesuit Missionaries, 1610-1791*, 73 vols. (Cleveland: Burrows Brothers, 1901), 6:297, 299.

Chapter 3: Making the first American West

Leader of the Indian confederacy rejects an offer from American diplomats to buy their land in 1793: E. A. Cruikshank, ed., *The Correspondence of Lieut. Governor John Graves Simcoe: With allied documents relating to his administration of the government of Upper Canada*, 5 vols. (Toronto: Ontario Historical Society, 1923-1931), 2:19.

George Washington on acquiring Western lands: Washington quoted in Bernard Bailyn, *Voyagers to the West: A Passage in the Peopling of America on the Eve of the Revolution* (New York: Knopf, 1986), 23.

Thomas Gage on the similarities between Western Pennsylvanians and Indians: Lieut.-General Thomas Gage to Earl of Hillsborough, Oct. 7, 1772, in K. G. Davies, ed., *Documents of the American Revolution, 1770-1783*, 21 vols. (Shannon: Irish University Press, 1972-81), 5:203.

Sir William Johnson on ungovernable backcountry people: Sir William Johnson to Earl of Dartmouth, September 22, 1773, in K. G. Davies, ed., *Documents of the American Revolution, 1770–1783*, 21 vols. (Shannon: Irish University Press, 1972–81), 6:225.

George Washington on the Transylvania Company's purchase of Kentucky lands: Washington quoted in William Stewart Lester, *The Transylvania Colony* (Spencer, IN: Samuel R. Guard, 1935), 41.

Captain Pipe's speech to British officials: James H. O'Donnell III, ed., "Captain Pipe's Speech: A Commentary on the Delaware Experience, 1775–1781," *Northwest Ohio Quarterly* 64 (1992): 131.

Thomas Jefferson on agrarian expansion: Thomas Jefferson, *Notes on the State of Virginia* (Richmond: J. W. Randolph, 1853), 176.

Chapter 4: Taking the farther West

Governor Pio Pico on immigration into California: Pico quoted in Douglas Monroy, *Thrown among Strangers: The Making of Mexican Culture in Frontier California* (Berkeley: University of California Press, 1990), 163.

Meriwether Lewis and William Clark on fulfilling the task given to them by Thomas Jefferson: Lewis, journal entry, February 14, 1806, in Gary Moulton, ed., *The Journals of Lewis and Clark*, at "The Journals of the Lewis and Clark Expedition" website, http://lewisandclarkjournals.unl.edu/read/?_xmlsrc=1806-02-14&_xslsrc=LCstyles.xsl, accessed on August 1, 2014.

Thomas Hart Benton on the removal of Indians: Thomas Hart Benton, *Thirty Years' View; Or, A History of the Working of the American Government for Thirty Years, from 1820 to 1850*, 2 vols. (New York: D. Appleton, 1854–56), 1:28.

United Nations definition of "ethnic cleansing": quoted in John Mack Faragher, *A Great and Noble Scheme: The Tragic Story of the Expulsion of the French Acadians from Their American Homeland* (New York: Norton, 2005), 469.

Polk asking Congress to declare war on Mexico: Polk quoted in Daniel Walker Howe, *What Hath God Wrought: The Transformation of America, 1815–1848* (New York: Oxford University Press, 2007), 741.

Editor of a Democratic Party–aligned newspaper in 1845 on the United States' manifest destiny: John O'Sullivan, "Annexation," *United States Magazine and Democratic Review* 17, no. 1 (July-August 1845): 5.

Trist on the war with Mexico: Trist quoted in Amy S. Greenberg, *A Wicked War: Polk, Lincoln, and the 1846 Invasion of Mexico* (New York: Knopf, 2012), 259.

Chapter 5: The whitening of the West

De la Guerra on the word "white": de la Guerra quoted in Ross
    J. Browne, *Report of the Debate in the Convention of California, on
    the Formation of the State Constitution, in September and October,
    1849* (Washington, DC: John T. Powers, 1850), 64.

The superintendent of one reservation explains how reformation
    can ensure Indian survival: superintendent Clark Thompson
    quoted in David A. Nichols, *Lincoln and the Indians: Civil War
    Policy and Politics* (Columbia: University of Missouri Press,
    1978), 180.

On sending Indian children to white boarding schools: Frederick
    E. Hoxie, *A Final Promise: The Campaign to Assimilate the
    Indians, 1880–1920* (Lincoln: University of Nebraska Press,
    1984), 67.

Henry Dawes on the Dawes Act: Dawes quoted in Patricia Nelson
    Limerick, *The Legacy of Conquest: The Unbroken Past of the
    American West* (New York: Norton, 1987), 198.

For the text of the Treaty of Guadalupe Hidalgo, see "The Avalon
    Project: Documents in Law, History, and Diplomacy," Yale Law
    School, http://avalon.law.yale.edu/19th_century/guadhida.asp,
    accessed on August 1, 2014.

Chapter 6: The watering of the West

Thomas Jefferson's prediction that the West would secure the agrarian
    character of the United States: Barbara B. Oberg, ed., *The Papers of
    Thomas Jefferson*, vol. 33, *17 February to 30 April 1801* (Princeton,
    NJ: Princeton University Press, 2006), 150.

Farming in the Great Plains in dry years and going bust: Joanna
    L. Stratton, *Pioneer Women: Voices from the Kansas Frontier*
    (New York: Simon and Schuster, 1981), 12.

Theodore Roosevelt on nationalizing irrigation projects: Roosevelt
    quoted in William Cronon, "Landscapes of Abundance and
    Scarcity," in Clyde A. Milner II, Carol A. O'Connor, and Martha
    A. Sandweiss, eds., *The Oxford History of the American West*
    (New York: Oxford University Press, 1994), 618.

John Muir on the damming of Hetch Hetchy: Muir quoted in Donald
    Worster, *A Passion for Nature: The Life of John Muir* (New York:
    Oxford University Press, 2008), 425.

Chapter 7: The worldly West

The *Wall Street Journal* on the 1965 Immigration Reform Act: *Wall Street Journal* quoted in Sarah Deutsch, George J. Sánchez, and Gary Okihiro, "Contemporary Peoples/Contested Places," in Clyde A. Milner II, Carol A. O'Connor, and Martha A. Sandweiss, eds., *The Oxford History of the American West* (New York: Oxford University Press, 1994), 646.

Chapter 8: The view from Hollywood

Sergio Leone on Westerns: Christopher Frayling Interview with Sergio Leone, in Christopher Frayling, *Once upon a Time in Italy: The Westerns of Sergio Leone* (New York: Abrams in association with the Autry National Center, 2005), 88.

1939 report by a federal housing agency on Boyle Heights: Home Owners Loan Corporation City Survey Files, quoted in George J. Sánchez, "'What's Good for Boyle Heights Is Good for the Jews': Creating Multiculturalism on the Eastside during the 1950s," *American Quarterly* 56 (2004): 637.

For video of Rodney King's 1992 plea, see "Can We All Just Get Along? For the Kids & Old People? Rodney King Speaks," https://www.youtube.com/watch?v=1sONfxPCTU0. accessed on August 1, 2014.

Theodore Roosevelt on manifest destiny: Theodore Roosevelt, *Thomas Hart Benton* (Boston: Houghton, Mifflin, 1886), 35, 40, 175.

Further reading

Overviews

Deverell, William. *A Companion to the American West*. Malden, MA:
    Blackwell, 2004.

Hine, Robert V., and John Mack Faragher. *The American West: A New
    Interpretive History*. New Haven, CT: Yale University Press, 2000.

Lamar, Howard, ed. *The New Encyclopedia of the American West*.
    New Haven, CT: Yale University Press, 1998.

Limerick, Patricia N. *The Legacy of Conquest: The Unbroken Past of
    the American West*. New York: Norton, 1987.

Milner, Clyde, Carol O'Connor, and Martha Sandweiss, eds. *The Oxford
    History of the American West*. New York: Oxford University Press,
    1994.

Nugent, Walter. *Into the West: The Story of Its People*. New York:
    Knopf, 1999.

Turner, Frederick Jackson. *The Frontier in American History*.
    New York: Holt, 1920.

White, Richard. *"It's Your Misfortune and None of My Own": A New
    History of the American West*. Norman: University of Oklahoma
    Press, 1991.

Chapters 1: The view from Cahokia and 2: Empires and enclaves

Calloway, Colin G. *One Vast Winter Count: The Native American West
    before Lewis and Clark*. Lincoln: University of Nebraska Press, 2003.

Crosby, Alfred W., Jr. *Ecological Imperialism: The Biological Expansion
    of Europe, 900–1900*. New York: Cambridge University Press, 1986.

Hämäläinen, Pekka. *The Comanche Empire*. New Haven, CT: Yale University Press, 2008.

Mann, Charles C. *1491: New Revelations of the Americas before Columbus*. New York: Knopf, 2005.

Pauketat, Timothy R. *Cahokia: Ancient America's Great City on the Mississippi*. New York: Viking Penguin, 2009.

Richter, Daniel. *Before the Revolution: America's Ancient Pasts*. Cambridge, MA: Harvard University Press, 2011.

Taylor, Alan. *American Colonies: The Settling of North America*. New York: Penguin, 2001.

Weber, David J. *The Spanish Frontier in North America*. New Haven, CT: Yale University Press, 1994.

White, Richard. *The Middle Ground: Indians, Empires, and Republics in the Great Lakes Region, 1650–1815*. New York: Cambridge University Press, 1991.

Chapter 3: Making the first American West

Aron, Stephen. *How the West Was Lost: The Transformation of Kentucky from Daniel Boone to Henry Clay*. Baltimore: Johns Hopkins University Press, 1996.

Faragher, John Mack. *Daniel Boone: The Life and Legend of an American Pioneer*. New York: Holt, 1992.

Nugent, Walter. *Habits of Empire: A History of American Expansion*. New York: Knopf, 2008.

Rohrbough, Malcolm J. *Trans-Appalachian Frontier: People, Societies, and Institutions, 1775–1850*. Bloomington: Indiana University Press, 2008.

Chapter 4: Taking the farther West

Aron, Stephen. *American Confluence: The Missouri Frontier from Borderland to Border State*. Bloomington: Indiana University Press, 2006.

Delay, Brian. *War of a Thousand Deserts: Indian Raids and the U.S.-Mexican War*. New Haven, CT: Yale University Press, 2008.

Hyde, Anne. *Empires, Nations, and Families: A New History of the North American West, 1800–1860*. Lincoln: University of Nebraska Press, 2011.

Rohrbough, Malcolm J. *Days of Gold: The California Gold Rush and the American Nation*. Berkeley: University of California Press, 1997.

Unruh, John D. *The Plains Across: The Overland Emigrants and the Trans-Mississippi West, 1840–1860*. Champaign: University of Illinois Press, 1979.

Chapter 5: The whitening of the West

Brown, Richard Maxwell. *No Duty to Retreat: Violence and Values in American History and Society*. New York: Oxford University Press, 1991.

Graybill, Andrew. *Policing the Plains: Rangers, Mounties, and the North American Frontier, 1875–1910*. Lincoln: University of Nebraska Press, 2007.

Jacoby, Karl. *Shadows at Dawn: A Borderlands Massacre and the Violence of History*. New York: Penguin, 2008.

West, Elliott. *The Contested Plains: Indians, Goldseekers, and the Rush to Colorado*. Lawrence: University Press of Kansas, 1998.

Chapter 6: The watering of the West

Andrews, Thomas. *Killing for Coal: America's Deadliest Labor War*. Cambridge, MA: Harvard University Press, 2008.

Hundley, Norris, Jr. *The Great Thirst: Californians and Water: A History*. Rev. ed. Berkeley: University of California Press, 2001.

White, Richard. *Railroaded: The Transcontinentals and the Making of Modern America*. New York: Norton, 2011.

Worster, Donald. *Rivers of Empire: Water, Aridity, and the Growth of the American West*. New York: Oxford University Press, 1985.

Chapter 7: The worldly West

Barkan, Elliott. *From All Points: America's Immigrant West, 1870–1952*. Bloomington: Indiana University Press, 2007.

Gregory, James N. *The Southern Diaspora: How the Great Migrations of Black and White Southerners Transformed America*. Chapel Hill: University of North Carolina Press, 2005.

Pomeroy, Earl. *The American Far West in the Twentieth Century*. New Haven, CT: Yale University Press, 2008.

Taylor, Quintard. *In Search of the Racial Frontier: African Americans in the American West, 1528–1990*. New York: Norton, 1998.

Chapter 8: The view from Hollywood

Avila, Eric. *Popular Culture in the Age of White Flight: Fear and Fantasy in Suburban Los Angeles.* Berkeley: University of California Press, 2004.

Braudy, Leo. *The Hollywood Sign: Fantasy and Reality of an American Icon.* New Haven, CT: Yale University Press, 2011.

Davis, Mike. *City of Quartz: Excavating the Future in Los Angeles.* London: Verso, 1990.

Slotkin, Richard. *Gunfighter Nation: The Myth of the Frontier in Twentieth-Century America.* New York: Atheneum, 1992.

Stevenson, Brenda. *The Contested Murder of Latasha Harlins: Justice, Gender, and the L.A. Riots.* New York: Oxford University Press, 2013.

Index

Index

Y